THE SCHOOLS HISTORY PROJECT
· S·H·P ·
· OFFICIAL TEXT ·

E S S E N Ļ I A L

THE AMERICAN WEST 1840–1895
THE STRUGGLE FOR THE PLAINS

a study in depth

DAVE MARTIN
NIGEL WATT

HODDER
EDUCATION
A HACHETTE UK COMPANY

The Schools History Project

Set up in 1972 to bring new life to history for students aged 13–16, the Schools History Project continues to play an innovatory role in secondary history education. From the start, SHP aimed to show how good history has an important contribution to make to the education of a young person. It does this by creating courses and materials which both respect the importance of up-to-date, well-researched history and provide enjoyable learning experiences for students.

Since 1978 the Project has been based at Trinity and All Saints University College Leeds. It continues to support, inspire and challenge teachers through the annual conference, regional courses and website: http://www.schoolshistoryproject.org.uk. The Project is also closely involved with government bodies and awarding bodies in the planning of courses for Key Stage 3, GCSE and A level.

Note: The wording and sentence structure of some written sources have been adapted and simplified to make them accessible to all students, while faithfully preserving the sense of the original.

Words printed in SMALL CAPITALS are defined in the Glossary on page 92–93.

Acknowledgements

Photos

Cover and p.2 Museum of the City of New York/Bridgeman Art Library; **p.5** © Tom Bean/Corbis; **p.10** Peter Newark's American Pictures; **p.11** Private Collection/Bridgeman Art Library; **p.16** Smithsonian American Art Museum/Art Resource/Scala, Florence; **p.17** courtesy Department of Library Services, American Museum of Natural History (photo by Logan); **p.22** Private Collection/Christie's Images/Bridgeman Art Library; **p.23** Peter Newark's American Pictures; **p.30** The Bancroft Library; **p.32** National Portrait Gallery Smithsonian/Art Resource/Scala, Florence; **p.33** The Denver Public Library, Western History Collection; **p.34** © Bettmann/Corbis; **p.39** Nebraska State Historical Society (nbhips 10358); **p.41** Nebraska State Historical Society (nbhips 10527); **p.44** The Kansas State Historical Society, Topeka, Kansas; **p.45** *t* © Corbis, *b* Peter Newark's American Pictures; **p.49** *l & r* Peter Newark's American Pictures; **p.50** The Montana Historical Society, Helena; **p.55** Peter Newark's American Pictures; **p.64** Peter Newark's American Pictures; **p.67** American Heritage Center, University of Wyoming, Laramie; **p.71** *t & b* Peter Newark's American Pictures; **p.72** Smithsonian Institution neg. no. 3195-G; **p.76** *t* courtesy Eric von Schmidt, copyright 1976 world wide rights reserved, *b* Whitney Gallery of Western Art, Cody, WY/Bridgeman Art Library; **p.80** Burton Historical Collection, Detroit Public Gallery; **p.82** Smithsonian Institution, neg. no. 56630; **p.84** *l* Smithsonian Institution, neg. no. 57489, *r* Smithsonian Institution, neg. no. 57490; **p.85** Nebraska State Historical Society.

Every effort has been made to trace all copyright holders, but if any have been inadvertently overlooked the publishers will be pleased to make the necessary arrangements at the earliest opportunity.

Although every effort has been made to ensure that website addresses are correct at time of going to press, Hodder Education cannot be held responsible for the content of any website mentioned in this book. It is sometimes possible to find a relocated web page by typing in the address of the home page for a website in the URL window of your browser.

Orders: please contact Bookpoint Ltd, 130 Milton Park, Abingdon, Oxon OX14 4SB. Telephone: (44) 01235 827720. Fax: (44) 01235 400454. Lines are open 9.00–5.00, Monday to Saturday, with a 24-hour message answering service. Visit our website at www.hoddereducation.co.uk

© Dave Martin, Nigel Watt, 2005

First published in 2005 by
Hodder Education, an Hachette UK company,
338 Euston Road
London NW1 3BH

Impression number   10 9 8
Year   2013

Layouts by Fiona Webb
Artwork by Art Construction, Jon Davis/Linden Artists, Richard Duszczak, Tony Randell, Steve Smith, Malcolm Stokes/Linden Artists.
Typeset in 10.5/12pt Walbaum by Phoenix Photosetting, Chatham, Kent
Printed and bound in Dubai

A catalogue record for this title is available from the British Library
ISBN 9780719577550   Teacher's Resource Book
ISBN: 9780719577567

Contents

There is a lot going on in this painting. On the left are the American settlers. They are building towns, roads and railways as they expand onto the Great Plains. On the right are the Plains Indians who lived on the Great Plains. They are choking on the smoke of the train. But a lot more than their lungs was at stake. Their whole way of life and the land they lived on was about to become a battleground. This book examines this struggle for control of the Great Plains. You will investigate:

Why did other people want to move onto the Plains?

In chapter 2 find out who else wanted to live on the Plains and why. Then discover which group of settlers had the most impact on the Indian way of life.

How did the Plains Indians live on the Great Plains?

In chapter 1 find out about the way of life of the Plains Indians and judge how successfully they learned to live on the Plains.

Your pathway

■ ACTIVITY

There are four investigations in this book. Here they are shown as your pathway. One of your tasks as you work through this book is to choose a good image to go with each one. As you study each investigation choose what *you think* is the best picture to sum up each section. You will pull your ideas together at the end of the book.

Why was there conflict between the settlers and the Indians?

Finally, in chapter 4, find out why war broke out between the US government and the Plains Indians, who won, and why.

Was the West really lawless?

In chapter 3 investigate the battles that the settlers had with each other.

These are the **big questions** that you are going to answer in this book. To answer them you need to study the period in depth. A depth study:

■ concentrates on a short period of history – in this case only 55 years, 1840–1895
■ looks at one particular place at that time – in this case the American West
■ looks at the lives of ordinary children, women and men – not just at famous or powerful people
■ studies people's feelings and motives – what made them tick and why they did what they did.

exam BUSTERS

... and at the same time as all that ...
Exam Busters will help you develop skills you need to succeed at GCSE. Featuring:

■  Find out what examiners are really looking for.

■ Spot the good points in someone's answer and see if you can improve the bad points.

■ Learn how to avoid easy mistakes.

■ **smarter REVISION** Learn how to remember important information and revise effectively.

1.1 *The Great American Desert?*

On some old maps of North America the Great Plains were marked as 'The Great American Desert'. People thought no one could live there. They were wrong. Find out what the Great Plains were really like, who lived there and why.

The Great Plains

▼ **SOURCE 1** A map of North America showing the location and characteristics of the Great Plains in 1840

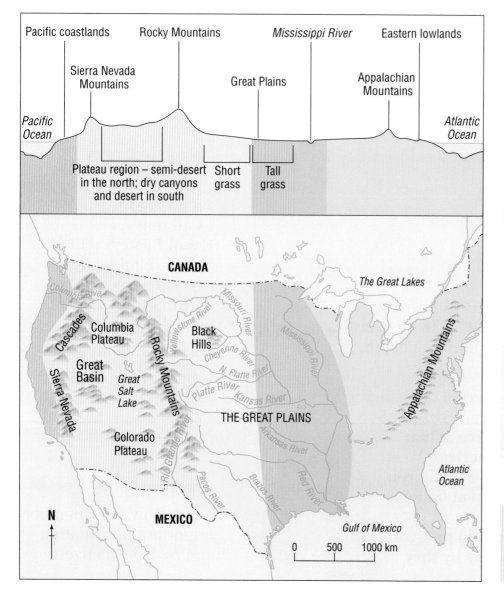

Landscape
This was a region of gently rolling grasslands and slow flowing rivers. To the north were the Black Hills, wooded hills surrounded by the 'Badlands', where soft rock was eroded into fantastic shapes.

Climate
The climate was one of extremes of temperature with strong winds all year. In winter these winds brought blizzards and freezing cold. In summer they were very hot, drying up the land and rivers.

Vegetation
The majority was grassland. In some of the river valleys and close to the Mississippi there was woodland. Berries, root plants and wild fruit grew in some places.

Wildlife
There was a range of animals and birds. Most common were the great herds of buffalo.

▼ **SOURCE 2** Major Stephen Long's description of the Great Plains, 1819–1820

In regard to this country, I do not hesitate in giving my opinion that it is almost wholly unfit for cultivation, and of course uninhabitable by a people depending upon farming for their SUBSISTENCE. *Large areas of fertile land are to be found, but the scarcity of wood and water will prove an impossible obstacle in the way of settling the country.*

■ **ACTIVITY**

1 Study Source 2. Your teacher can give you a copy. Major Long points out that the Great Plains are unsuitable for cultivation so people who depend on farming cannot live there. Highlight the words where he writes this.

2 Major Long does suggest that some land is fertile or suitable for farming, but there is a second problem that will stop people from settling there. What is this problem? Again, highlight the key words.

▼ **SOURCE 3** A photograph of the Great Plains

Who was living there and why?

The Great Plains were not empty. There were people, the Plains Indians, living there before explorers like Major Stephen Long arrived. At first the Indians lived in the east of America, but by the 1700s many began to move west.

▼ **SOURCE 4** A map of the Plains showing the locations of some of the Indian nations in 1840

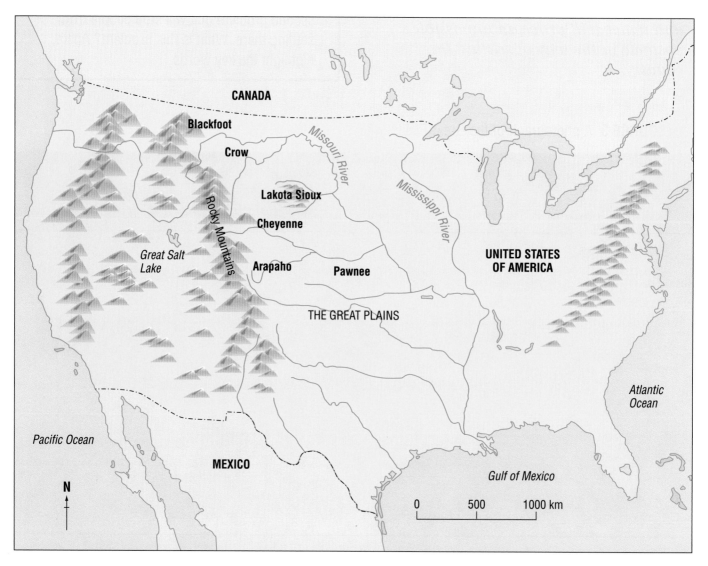

Rather than study every Plains Indian NATION you will focus on just one, the Lakota Sioux. Can you find them in Source 4?

▼ **SOURCE 5** Factors that explain why the Sioux moved onto the Plains

■ **ACTIVITY**

Source 5 is an illustration of the four factors that explain why the Sioux moved west onto the Plains. Underneath it are four caption cards. Match each of the caption cards to the correct illustration.

■ **DISCUSS**

What problems do you think the Sioux might face when they moved to live on the Plains?

Push factor 1
The Sioux faced the threat of attack from other Indian nations and pressure from settlers moving in from the East. These better-armed newcomers *pushed* the Sioux to move west.

Push factor 2
The new settlers brought diseases with them. These diseases, like measles, were fatal to the Sioux. This *pushed* the Sioux to move west.

Enabling factor
The Sioux owned horses that allowed, or *enabled*, them to travel freely across the long distances of the Plains.

Pull factor
The Plains were empty of other people, but full of buffalo. This *pulled* the Sioux onto the Plains.

1.2 *Culture shock!*

The white Americans who first met the Sioux on the Plains found that they lived very different lives from their own. This sometimes led them to see the Sioux as uncivilised savages. You will examine these views and sum up your own first impressions of the Sioux.

My name is **Full Moon**. I am a member of the Sioux nation. The whole Sioux nation does not live together. There are too many of us. Instead we live, work and travel in small BANDS. My husband, White Cloud, lives with my family. That is the custom. Ours was a love marriage. White Cloud gave my father four horses and ten buffalo HIDES!

I hope he becomes even richer so that he can take another wife. It would be good to have someone to share the work with. I look after our TIPI, prepare food, fetch water and make all our clothing. My mother taught me all these skills and I enjoy my work. Do you like this deer skin shirt I am sewing for White Cloud?

My name is **White Cloud**, I am married to Full Moon. As a warrior and hunter it is my job to feed and protect my family and band. I learned my skill with horses and weapons from my father. It's a good job I did. Before I married Full Moon she sang to me:

You may go on the warpath
When your name I hear
Having done something brave
Then I will marry you.

Along with the rest of the men in our band I sit in council. We smoke the medicine pipe to ask the Great Spirit for wisdom. We make the important decisions about where to position our village, when to move and when we should raid our enemies, the Pawnee. We usually follow the advice of our chief, Many Buffalo, but the opinions of the old men are always listened to with great respect.

▼ **SOURCE 1** An extract from George Catlin's book, *Manners, Customs and Condition of the North American Indians*, published in 1841. Catlin travelled on the Plains for many years and recorded the lives of the Plains Indians in words and paintings. But he was always a white outsider, judging them by his own values and beliefs. Here he describes Sioux marriage

The son of this chief, a youth of eighteen years, and whose portrait I painted, distinguished himself by taking four wives in one day! *... I visited the* tipi *of this young man several times, and saw his four modest little wives seated around the fire, where all were entering very happily on the duties and pleasures of married life. The ages of these young brides were probably all between twelve and fifteen years. There is a more early approach to maturity in this country than in* **CIVILISED** *communities ... In this country* **POLYGAMY** *is allowed, for where there are two or three times the number of women than there are men, such an arrangement answers a good purpose, for so many females are taken care of.*

▼ **SOURCE 2** A second extract from Catlin's book in which he describes the treatment of one very old man

When we were about to start on our way from the village, my attention was directed to a very aged man, who was to be left behind ... a man who had once been a chief, who was now too old to travel. 'My children', he said, 'our nation is poor, and it is necessary that you should all go to the country where you can get meat. My eyes are dimmed and my strength is no more. My days are nearly all numbered, and I am a burden to my children. I cannot go and I wish to die.'

This cruel custom of exposing their aged people belongs, I think, to all the tribes who roam about the prairies ...

■ ACTIVITY

Work with a partner. One of you complete Part A and the other complete Part B. Then work together on Part C.

Part A
1 Read Full Moon's words on page 8. Write down some key words to summarise what she says about Sioux marriage.
2 a) Now read Source 1. Write down some key words to summarise what George Catlin says about Sioux marriage.
   b) What tone does he use in his description? Pick out the most important phrase.
3 Compare the two accounts of Sioux marriage. What differences can you find?

Part B
1 Read White Cloud's words on page 8. Write down some key words to summarise what he says about the way the Sioux treat older people.
2 Now read Source 2. How does George Catlin describe the treatment of older people? Summarise his views with some key words.
3 Compare the two accounts of the way the Sioux treat older people. What differences can you find?

Part C
4 Now compare the notes that you have made with your partner. Consider:
   • what impression of Sioux life you have from the accounts of Full Moon and White Cloud
   • what impression of Sioux life you have from Catlin's accounts
   • how you think Sioux life differs to your own way of life.
5 Finally, each write a paragraph to sum up your own first impressions of the Sioux.

1.3 *How to survive on the Plains part 1: the buffalo*

In this unit you are going to look at how the way of life of the Plains Indians was well suited to living on the Plains. At the end you will make your own revision cards to sum up the main ideas.

In part one you are going to find out how life on the Plains for the Indians would have been impossible without the buffalo. You are going to examine how the Sioux hunted the buffalo and how they used *every part of it*.

Hunting the buffalo

The buffalo hunt is a very important part of our lives. Before each hunt we dance to call on the Great Spirit to help us. Then we send out SCOUTS to find the buffalo herds. Once they are found we set out together to hunt on horseback. Each hunter's arrows are marked so that he can identify the buffalo that he has personally killed. It is important to gain a reputation as a skilled and daring hunter.

To kill a buffalo you have to get close, very close. They are big and dangerous, very dangerous. That's what makes the hunt so exciting!

White Cloud

▼ **SOURCE 1** *Buffalo Dance of the Sioux*, painted by George Catlin. The Buffalo Dance was a religious ceremony to call on the help of the Great Spirit

Spear

Bow and arrow

'Buffalo' being killed

Drum and rattle

Men dressed as buffalo with buffalo heads and tails

■ **ACTIVITY**

Source 1 has been labelled to draw attention to the details. On your own copy of Source 2 label the following:

■ the weapons being used
■ the dead buffalo
■ the horse that has been brought down
■ the wounded buffalo attacking a horse
■ the hunter trying to leap to safety
■ the dismounted rider taking aim.

▼ **SOURCE 2** *Buffalo Hunt, Chase*, painted by George Catlin

■ **DISCUSS**

1 What were the dangers of buffalo hunting?
2 What can you learn about Indian religious beliefs from White Cloud's words and from Source 1?
3 Use Source 3 to explain why it was a great honour for young men to be chosen to take part in the buffalo hunt.

▼ **SOURCE 3** Black Elk, a Sioux born around 1863, describes the preparations for a hunt

Then the crier shouted, 'Your knives shall be sharpened. Make ready, make haste, your horses make ready! We shall go forth with arrows. Plenty of meat we shall make!'

Then the head man went around picking out the best hunters with the fastest horses. To these he said, 'Young warriors, your work I know is good; so today you will feed the helpless. You shall help the old and the young and whatever you kill shall be theirs'. This was a great honour for young men.

Using the buffalo

After the hunt we women go to work on the dead buffalo. The men get the excitement and we get the hard work. You can see two of my women friends, below. Little Elk is scraping a hide. This hide will later be sewn together with others to make a *tipi*. My other friend, Still Water, is hanging buffalo meat on a frame for drying. This preserves the meat. Almost everything in our village is made from some part of the buffalo.

Full Moon

▼ **SOURCE 4** A modern artist's illustration of a Sioux village

▼ **SOURCE 5** A hundred uses? How the Plains Indians used some other parts of the buffalo

Horns were used for arrow-straighteners, cups, fire-carriers, head-dress ornaments, ladles, spoons, toys and quill-flatteners.

The **flesh** was cooked, or dried and mixed with fat and wild cherries to preserve it as pemmican. **Intestines** were used for buckets and cooking vessels.

Bones were used for arrowheads, dice, game counters, jewellery, knives, needles, paint brushes, shovels, tools and war clubs.

The **organs** were cut from the body and left on the ground to give new life to the herd. The buffalo was sacred, man's relative who gave his life so that the people could live. The **heart** might also be eaten raw so that the warrior could take the strength and power of the buffalo. **Gall** from the **gall bladder** was used to make yellow paint. The **liver** was eaten raw as a delicacy.

The **brain** was used for tanning the hides.

Tanned hide was used for bags, belts, containers, horse harnesses, lashings, masks, sheaths, shields, snow-shoes, string, bedding, blankets, BULL BOATS, clothes, dolls, dresses, drums, leggings, mittens, MOCCASINS, pouches, robes, saddle and *tipi* covers.

Fur was used for decoration on clothes, as stuffing for saddles and pillows, and to make mittens and rope.

Dung was used for fuel (buffalo chips) and smoked by men in special ceremonies.

Hooves were used to make glue and also to make rattles and tools.

■ **ACTIVITY**

1 Compare Source 5 with Source 4. How many examples of the use of the buffalo can you find in Full Moon's village?
2 Why do you think there are images of the buffalo hunt on the *tipi*?
3 Would you describe the buffalo as **important** or **vital** to the Sioux way of life? Explain your choice.

Acronyms

■ **Why BIT = ABC can help you to remember the uses of the buffalo**

For your GCSE you need to develop your recall skills. If you are answering a question about how important the buffalo was to the Plains Indians you will need to support your answer. But you don't need to list 100 uses, just three is enough.

So how do you remember three parts of the buffalo and what they were used for? Inventing acronyms can help! A BIT of a buffalo could provide the Sioux with weapons, utensils and clothing.

> **BIT = ABC**
> **B**ones = **A**rrowheads
> **I**ntestines = **B**uckets
> **T**anned hides = **C**lothes

■ **ACTIVITY**

Invent a different acronym to help you remember the uses of the buffalo.

How to survive on the Plains part 2: the tipi

> We need to be able to move to follow the buffalo herds. So we never stay in one place for very long. That is why we live in *tipis*. We women make the *tipis* from buffalo hides. We own them. We put them up and we take them down.
>
> We have a proverb: 'A beautiful *tipi* is like a good mother. She hugs her children to her and protects them from heat and cold, snow and rain.'

▼ **SOURCE 6** A modern artist's illustration of a *tipi*. In summer the *tipi* bottom could be rolled up to let cool air in and in winter it could be banked with earth to help keep the *tipi* warm

▼ **SOURCE 7** Flying Hawk compares the *tipi* to the houses built by white settlers

The white man builds big house, cost much money, shut out sun, can never move. The tipi *is much better to live in: always clean, warm in winter, cool in summer, easy to move.*

▼ **SOURCE 8** Colonel Richard Dodge, a US army officer who served on the Plains in the 1830s, learned about the Indians, but did not fully understand them

The home or lodge ... is from twelve to twenty feet in diameter, and about fifteen feet high. The fire is built in the centre, and the smoke escapes through an opening at the top ... the lodge is usually in cold weather too full of smoke to be bearable to anyone but an Indian. It is, however, well adapted to their needs. Its shape secures it from the danger of being overturned by windstorms, and with very little fuel it can be kept warm and comfortable even in the coldest weather.

The beds are piles of buffalo robes and blankets, spread on the ground ... They serve as sleeping places by night, and seats by day. In this small space are often crowded eight or ten persons, possibly of three or four different families. Since the cooking, eating, living and sleeping are all done in the one room it soon becomes unbelievably filthy.

■ DISCUSS

You are going to role-play a discussion between Flying Hawk and Colonel Dodge about the strengths and weaknesses of a *tipi* as a home for Plains Indians. Your teacher can give you copies of Sources 7 and 8.

Flying Hawk

1 If you are going to play the part of Flying Hawk then think about Full Moon's words at the top of page 14 and carefully read Source 7. Can you find the positive points he makes? Either highlight them on your copy or note them down.

2 Flying Hawk also criticises settlers' houses. Find his three criticisms. Highlight them in a different colour on your copy or note them down.

Colonel Dodge

1 If you are going to play the part of Colonel Dodge then carefully read Source 8. Find three criticisms of the *tipi* that Colonel Dodge makes. Highlight them on your copy or note them down.

2 Can you think of anything else about the *tipi* that Colonel Dodge would have disliked if he had had to live in one?

3 However, he was not completely critical. Find the positive points he makes. Highlight them in a different colour on your copy, or note them down.

Now you are ready to discuss the *tipi*. Use your highlighting or notes to decide what to say.

Examine that question

exam BUSTERS

Why did the Sioux live in *tipis*? Explain your answer using your own knowledge.

You may have to answer an 'explain' question like this in your exam. You only need to write a single paragraph. Begin with a topic sentence like this:

... Sioux Indians lived in tipis because they were the best sort of housing for their needs on the Plains.

Then explain why *tipis* were the best sort of housing. You can do this by describing some of the problems the Sioux faced living on the Plains and then explain exactly how the *tipi* solved each problem. So your next four sentences might be:

Indians faced several problems living on the Plains. For example, they had to move to follow the buffalo herds. So they needed a home that could be moved. The tipi was ideal as it could be taken down and moved quickly and easily.

Then you might go on:

Another problem on the Plains was the strong winds. The tipi was ...

! WARNING

DON'T WRITE TOO MUCH

Usually questions like this are worth only a few marks so **don't write too much**. **Make your point and support it** with two or three examples.

Now that you have studied this advice, use it to write your answer.

How to survive on the Plains part 3: warfare

> War is the way in which a warrior wins fame. We raid our enemies to capture horses and for honour. My horse fights with me and goes hungry with me. If he is to carry me in battle then he must know my heart and I must know his. Then we will be brothers. Hear my war song.
>
> Crow Indian
> You must watch your horses
> A horse thief
> Often
> Am I.

Warfare to the Sioux was not about long campaigns fought by large numbers of men. Instead, raids were made by small groups of warriors. Typically, raiding parties would set out from a village two or three times a year. Raids were never made in winter when snow covered the Plains. Wars were not fought to conquer land. Plains Indians did not believe that anyone could own land. Wars were fought in order to protect hunting and living space or to steal horses.

Individual warriors gained honour by 'counting coup' – getting close enough to touch an enemy rather than kill him. If the enemy were too many then a warrior would avoid fighting. There was no honour in dying bravely. A dead warrior could not provide for his family.

When the Sioux had to fight violent battles they would take the SCALPS of their dead enemies as evidence of their success. When an Indian took the scalp of his enemy he also took his spirit so he would not go into the afterlife. The Scalp Dance was a celebration and a chance to thank the Great Spirit for his help in battle.

■ DISCUSS

If you witnessed a Scalp Dance like the one shown in Source 9 would you think the Sioux were savages?

◄ **SOURCE 9** *Scalp Dance*, painted by George Catlin. The attitude of the Plains Indians to warfare was completely different from those of the early settlers and the soldiers sent to protect them. The settlers and soldiers thought scalping was barbaric and that avoiding fighting was cowardly. These different attitudes would be one cause of misunderstanding between the two groups

How to survive on the Plains part 4: religion

Another important part of the Sioux's life on the Plains was religion. You can read how it affected the daily lives of White Cloud and Full Moon on page 18.

The Sun Dance

The Sun Dance was the most famous Sioux religious ceremony. This was danced in order to get help or guidance from the spirit world.

▼ **SOURCE 10** An extract from George Catlin's book *Manners, Customs and Condition of the North American Indians,* published in 1841

*We found him naked, except for his breechcloth, **with splints or skewers run through the flesh on both breasts.** He was leaning back and **hanging with the weight of his body to the top of the pole**, which was fastened by a cord, which was tied to the splints. His feet were still upon the ground, supporting a small part of his weight, and he held in his left hand his favourite bow, and in his right, with a desperate grip, his MEDICINE BAG. In this condition with the blood trickling down over his body, which was covered in white and yellow clay, and **amidst a great crowd** who were looking on, sympathizing with and encouraging him, he was hanging and 'looking at the sun' without paying any attention to anyone. In the group that was reclining around him, were **several medicine men beating their drums and shaking their rattles and singing as loud as they could yell,** to encourage him and strengthen his heart to stand and look at the sun from its rising in the morning 'til its setting at night. Then, if his heart and his strength have not failed him, he is 'cut down', and receives the presents (which have been thrown into a pile before him during the day) and also the name of a doctor, or medicine man which lasts him and ensures him respect.*

▼ **SOURCE 11** *Sun Dance,* a painting by Short Bull. The Sun Dance took place inside a circle. The circle was sacred to the Sioux

■ **ACTIVITY**

Carefully read Source 10. Some words and phrases have been highlighted to help you. Now look closely at Source 11. In many religions the ceremonies have the same features:

- a CONGREGATION
- music
- holy objects
- priest(s)
- special places/buildings
- individual participants.

Can you find evidence of these in the Sun Dance of the Sioux?

Our beliefs are very important to us.
We believe in Wakan Tanka, the Great Spirit.
He created the world and everything in it.
All living creatures, animals, birds, fish and plants
as well as human beings, have a spirit. All should
try and live in harmony.
We contact Wakan Tanka in our ceremonies with
our singing and dancing.
And the land, well, that is sacred.
No one can own land.

One way we contact the spirits is through
visions. I had my first vision when I became a
woman. They guide us in our daily lives. And if
we are still unsure then we can go to a MEDICINE MAN
and ask his advice. When I was ill with pains in the
head our medicine man beat his drum to drive
the evil spirit out and gave me white willow bark
to chew. That worked.

A question of land

To the Plains Indians land was part of the circle of life
and death and many specific places, like the Black
Hills, were sacred to them. They believed that they
came from the land and they would return to the land.
They believed that the land could not be owned, bought
or sold by anyone. This became an important issue
when the Indians came into contact with the settlers.

Revision cards

smarter REVISION

As you know, for your GCSE you need to develop your recall skills so that you can remember important information. You have already made up an acronym. Now here is another technique, making a set of revision cards.

You are going to use all the work that you have done on the Indians' way of life to make a set of revision cards that explain **how the way of life of the Plains Indians was suited to living on the Plains**. The card on 'Moving' has been completed for you.

Each card explains an aspect of how the Plains Indians lived. Then this is given a score out of five to explain how important you think this aspect of life was to helping the Sioux survive on the Plains.

Now write cards on these two topics : the Sun Dance; the buffalo.

Keep your cards short with no more than two or three bullet points. You must be able to remember them!

As an extra memory prompt add an icon to each card.

exam BUSTERS

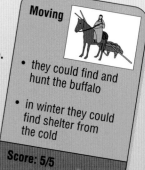

Moving

• they could find and hunt the buffalo

• in winter they could find shelter from the cold

Score: 5/5

Who was more important in Plains Indian society, men or women?

■ ACTIVITY

As a class, you are going to take part in a boxing match debate to answer the following question:

Who was more important in Plains Indian society, men or women?

This is how it works. Half the class forms a group to represent the women. The other half of the class forms a group to represent the men. In your group one of you will be the boxer, the rest will be their tacticians.

In your groups you need to look back over all of the work that you have done in this chapter and come up with three points that support your argument that women or men were more important.

Round 1...

- When the teacher rings the bell send your boxer forward. They now deliver your group's three points. Each one is a punch. The other side have to listen very carefully. They will need to come up with a good response for their boxer to answer each point if they are to block your punches.

- Next their boxer delivers their three points / punches. Now it's your turn to listen carefully and think how you will block their punches.

- Both boxers return to their corners. Each group now prepares their 'blocks' and further 'punches'. When the bell sounds send your boxer forward again. Are your blocks good enough? Will your punches land? Your teacher will decide and keep score.

Round 2...
And the winner is?

What decision did your class reach? Which boxer won? Record your conclusion on your own copy of one of the boxing belts below.

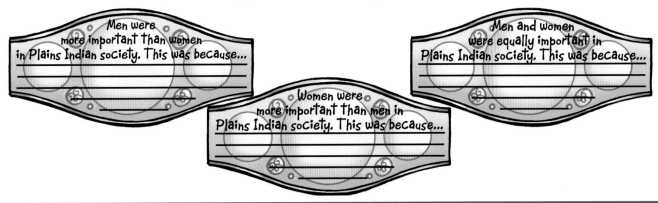

Men were more important than women in Plains Indian society. This was because...

Women were more important than men in Plains Indian society. This was because...

Men and women were equally important in Plains Indian society. This was because...

The lives of the Plains Indians

25 All
You have lived for many moons. Now it is time for you to record your life for the people who are to come.

24 Life or death
The buffalo hunting is poor. There is little food for the people. Many people die. Do you?

23 Life or death
Bluecoats attack your village. Many of the people are killed. Are you?

22 Female
Your husband is gored and killed during the buffalo hunt.

21 Male
You lose all five of your horses in a bet on a ball game.

20 All
You camp with the Oglala, Crazy Horse's Sioux band. It is a happy time with horse racing and other games.

6 All
In the Moon when Wolves Run Together, the snow is so deep that the men cannot hunt. The story telling is good.

5 Life or death
Your village is raided by the Pawnee. Are you killed in the fighting?

4 Female
Your mother teaches you how to do porcupine quill embroidery.

3 Male
You receive your first vision after a three-day fast.

19 Female
You gain a reputation as a skilled healer. People come to you for help.

7 All
In the Moon When Green Grass is Up, the buffalo hunting is good. No one will go hungry in your village this year.

2 Female
Your period starts. You now have the power to talk to the spirits.

18 Male
You are selected by the medicine man to hunt for the tribe, the old, young, the helpless. A great honour.

8 All
Your father, Little Bear, leads a successful raid against the Crow. The people have many horses.

1 Male
Your uncle teaches you how to break (train for riding) a pony.

17 Female
Your husband takes a second wife, your sister. You are pleased as now you can share the work.

9 Female
You are invited to join the quilling society as your skill is admired.

16 Male
Your offer of marriage is accepted by Full Moon's parents.

10 Male
You go on your first raid against the Crow. You look after the horses.

11 Life or death
The white man's sickness (smallpox) comes to your village. Many of the people die. It is a time of great sorrow.

12 Female
You pick berries with White Cloud. He plans to ask your parents for permission to marry you.

13 Male
You are invited to join the Kit Fox warrior society as your bravery is admired.

14 Male
You count coup for the first time on a Crow warrior.

15 Female
Your first child is born.

■ ACTIVITY

Play the game on page 20.
You and your partner should start by choosing whether to be male or female. Give yourselves names. You need to roll a dice to move around the board. Make notes about what happens to you as you move. Keep this as a diary. If you land on a life or death square you must roll the dice again. If you throw two or less, you die. If you do die, take a new name and start again.

▼ **SOURCE 1** An extract from George Catlin's book *Manners, Customs and Condition of the North American Indians*, 1841

The North American Indian in his native state is an honest, faithful, brave, warlike, cruel, revengeful, relentless – yet honourable, thoughtful and religious being.

■ DISCUSS

1 In Source 1 George Catlin was trying to sum up how he felt about the Plains Indians. Now that you have studied the different features of their lives, do you agree with him?
2 What were the two most important factors in enabling the Indians to live successfully on the Plains?

You ask me to plough the ground! Shall I take a knife and cut my mother's bosom? Then when I die she will not take me to her bosom to rest. You ask me to cut grass and make hay and sell it and be rich like white men. But how shall I dare cut off my mother's hair?

Coming up...
You have now studied a number of the features of the Plains Indians' way of life. Once settlers began to live on the Plains they had an effect on this lifestyle. Refer to your revision cards on how the Indians' lives were suited to the Plains, throughout Chapter 2. Think about how each aspect of their lives might be affected by the actions of the settlers.

Of course, the big issue was land. Remember that the Plains Indians believed land was sacred and could not be owned by anyone. What do you think their reaction would be to settlers farming the land and miners digging it for gold?

2.1 *What was America's 'Manifest Destiny'?*

MANIFEST DESTINY was an idea. It was an important idea because it encouraged many Americans to head west. Your task will be to write your own definition of Manifest Destiny.

You will also start the big task that will run through the whole of this chapter – to compare the settlers and decide which group had the greatest impact on the lives of the Plains Indians.

This chapter investigates how Americans changed the Great Plains. It started with a trickle of settlers. By the end of the century thousands of people were living on the Great Plains. A railroad ran across the continent. There were towns and cities, farms and mines. The wilderness had been tamed.

Behind these changes lay a popular idea. It was called 'Manifest Destiny'.

It said that **Americans** had a **duty** to **spread** their way of life across the entire continent. It was what **God wanted them to do**. Anyone who went to live in the deserted areas of the West was following their Manifest Destiny. If anyone stood in the way of Manifest Destiny, they were standing in God's way.

◄ **SOURCE 1** *American Progress*, painted by John Gast, 1872. The painting is encouraging people to follow their Manifest Destiny

■ DISCUSS

1 How do you think the idea of Manifest Destiny would influence the way many Americans treated the Plains Indians?

■ ACTIVITY

2 Look at Source 1. Find:

- the Great Plains and the Rockies
- the settlers
- the herd of buffalo
- the grizzly bear
- the lady
- the Plains Indians.

■ DISCUSS

Study Source 1.

3 How are the groups of settlers travelling?

4 What work are some of the settlers doing?

5 How are the Indians reacting to the settlers?

6 a) Describe the way the colours change across the painting.
b) Why do you think the artist used different colours in this way?

7 What is the lady in the centre of the painting carrying? What does this mean?

8 Why do you think John Gast called his painting *American Progress*?

■ WRITE

9 Write your own definition of Manifest Destiny. You can use the highlighted words in the second paragraph on page 22 to help you.

⭧ SETTLER GRIDS

As you work through this chapter use Settler Grids like the one shown here to keep a record of each group of settlers. Your teacher can give you copies. These will help you when you revise.
These are the groups you will study.

Mountain men	**Mormons**
Pioneers	**Homesteaders**
Gold miners	**Cattlemen and cowboys**

Group of settlers:			
Reasons why they headed west	**Problems that they faced**	**Ways they solved their problems**	**How they affected the Indians**

Column four will be the most difficult, so as you read about each group, look out for the Plains Indians. You will see them in some of the pictures. You will read about settlers who met them. Remember the important question: What impact did the settlers have on the Plains Indians?
At the end of this chapter you will be asked to decide which groups of settlers made the biggest impact on the Indians.

2.2 *Passing through: why did the early settlers cross the Plains?*

During the first half of the nineteenth century many Americans crossed the Plains to settle in the far west. They were not interested in the Plains themselves – they were just passing through. Over the next eight pages you will join the mountain men, the pioneers and the gold miners in their adventures. You will find out why they decided to head west. You will learn about the problems they faced and how they overcame them.

▼ **SOURCE 1** Mountain men at work

Group 1: the mountain men

Many fur companies employed trappers to hunt for beaver. There was money to be made because in the 1800s beaver felt hats had become popular in cities in the east of America.

When they had killed all the beaver in the East, the trappers looked to the forests and rivers of the Rocky Mountains for beaver. They became known as 'mountain men'.

Mountain men lived lonely lives. There were many who spent their whole lives in the mountains, using the land for food, shelter and to make a living. They set their own beaver traps and once or twice a year they travelled to the Mississippi River and sold their beaver skins to the fur companies. They enjoyed telling people about their adventures and the sights that they had seen. Sometimes they TRADED with Indians. Some even married Indians.

> I wonder if anyone will be interested when we tell them that we have found a new pass through the Rockies?

■ DISCUSS

1 Look out! The mountain men are in danger! What hazards and dangers can you find in Source 1?
2 Quick! Take action! What can the mountain men do to protect themselves? Look at Source 1 carefully!
3 Would you like to have lived the life of a mountain man? Compare your own opinion with others in your class.

A famous mountain man – Jed Smith

Jed Smith probably travelled further than any other mountain man. He was born in 1799 and started trapping beaver in 1821. He found the South Pass through the Rocky Mountains and became the first American to travel overland to California through the deserts of the South-West. Unlike many other mountain men, he neither smoked nor drank, and he was very religious. When he was attacked by a grizzly bear, Smith nearly lost an ear. It was sewn on by one of his companions! He was killed by Indians in 1831. (Is he in Source 1?)

This beaver pelt should fetch a good price when we reach the Mississippi!

⮂ SETTLER GRIDS

Use the information on these two pages to complete your Settler Grid on the mountain men.

Group 2: the pioneers

In the 1840s thousands of men, women and children packed their possessions onto wagons and EMIGRATED to Oregon and California. They were called the PIONEERS because they were the first large group to cross the continent and settle in the West.

Oregon and California only became part of the United States in the 1840s, and must have seemed a world away from the overcrowded areas of the east coast. So why did the pioneers go?

▼ **SOURCE 2** Reasons why the pioneers emigrated to Oregon and California

1 When the 1837 DEPRESSION hit New York I lost my job. There is no work for me in the East.

2 These east coast winters are bad for our health. We want to move because it is warmer in California.

3 I have heard the stories of the mountain men. The West sounds much more exciting than Ohio!

4 Too many people are moving into this state. It is overcrowded and there is not enough good farmland.

5 Dear Brother,
You must join us in Oregon. The land is fertile and the rivers are full of fish.

■ ACTIVITY

1 PUSH FACTORS are the bad things about the East that made the pioneers want to leave.
2 PULL FACTORS are the good things about the West that made the pioneers want to go there.

Use Source 2 to help you draw up a list of Push and Pull factors that explain why the pioneers emigrated to the West.

If you are asked in your exam to explain why the pioneers emigrated to Oregon and California, make sure that you explain at least one push factor and one pull factor.

Heading west!

When the pioneers set out for Oregon, they faced a journey of 3000 kilometres along trails that had only recently been discovered by mountain men. It was considered good going if they made it within six months. One person out of every ten would die before they reached their destination.

▼ **SOURCE 3** Map showing the journey to the West

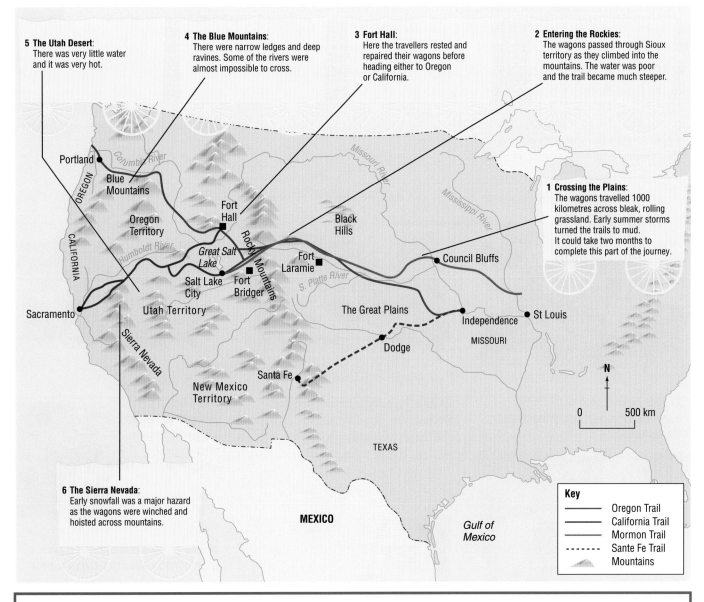

5 The Utah Desert:
There was very little water and it was very hot.

4 The Blue Mountains:
There were narrow ledges and deep ravines. Some of the rivers were almost impossible to cross.

3 Fort Hall:
Here the travellers rested and repaired their wagons before heading either to Oregon or California.

2 Entering the Rockies:
The wagons passed through Sioux territory as they climbed into the mountains. The water was poor and the trail became much steeper.

1 Crossing the Plains:
The wagons travelled 1000 kilometres across bleak, rolling grassland. Early summer storms turned the trails to mud. It could take two months to complete this part of the journey.

6 The Sierra Nevada:
Early snowfall was a major hazard as the wagons were winched and hoisted across mountains.

Portland
Blue Mountains
OREGON
Oregon Territory
CALIFORNIA
Columbia River
Fort Hall
Great Salt Lake
Humboldt River
Salt Lake City
Sacramento
Utah Territory
Sierra Nevada
New Mexico Territory
Santa Fe
Rocky Mountains
Fort Bridger
Fort Laramie
S. Platte River
Black Hills
The Great Plains
Dodge
Missouri River
Mississippi River
Council Bluffs
Independence
St Louis
MISSOURI
TEXAS
MEXICO
Gulf of Mexico

N

0   500 km

Key
——— Oregon Trail
——— California Trail
——— Mormon Trail
- - - - - Sante Fe Trail
▲▲▲ Mountains

■ **ACTIVITY**

3 Draw the routes of the trails on your own copy of Source 3 and highlight the most dangerous parts. Use pages 28–29 to help you.

■ **DISCUSS**

4 Which part of the journey would be the most difficult? Which part would be the most boring?

5 What sort of character would someone need to have, to be a pioneer?

Life on the trail

A pioneer family had to prepare for their journey carefully. They needed a strong, covered wagon, some oxen and enough equipment and supplies to last the journey. It was sensible to join others and become part of a larger wagon train.

In 1853, Mrs Amelia Stewart Knight travelled to Oregon with her husband, Joel, and their seven children whose ages ranged from three to seventeen. She kept a diary of her experiences on the trail (see Source 4).

▼ **SOURCE 4** Amelia Stewart Knight's journey to the West (actual quotes from Amelia's diary are shown in blue)

■ **DISCUSS**

What does Amelia Stewart Knight's diary (Source 4) tell you about:

a) the Indians
b) the role of women?

9 April Amelia's party began its journey. They travelled eight miles on the first day.

21 April
Rained all night; it is still raining. I have counted seventeen wagons travelling ahead of us in the mud and water.

7 June
We passed a large village of Sioux Indians. Some of the women had moccasins and beads, which they wanted to trade for bread.

21 June Amelia's party drank melted snow to survive, as they climbed through the Rockies.

28 June The party descended from the Rockies.
As far as the eye can see there is nothing but a sandy desert. The road is strewn with dead oxen and the stench is awful.

4 July Amelia's youngest son fell into a fever. He had been badly bitten by mosquitoes.

18 July Amelia was scared as the party entered the country of the Digger Indians.
I lay awake all night. I expected every minute we would be killed.

6 September To save weight in the Blue Mountains Amelia's party threw away some items and burnt the deck boards of the wagons.

9 September
Came through swamps, over rocks and hummocks [low hills] … There are wagons and chains lying all along this road.

Early October Amelia gave birth to her eighth child. Her husband bought a plot of land in Oregon and a small log cabin. The family had survived the Oregon Trail!

Not all of the pioneers were as lucky as the Knight family. Pioneers had to start their journeys before the end of April and any delays could be disastrous. In 1846 the Donner party failed to reach California because they were caught by early snowfalls in the Sierra Nevada, near the end of their journey. When they ran out of food some members of the party ate the flesh of their dead companions.

SETTLER GRIDS

Use the information from pages 26–29 to complete your Settler Grid on the pioneers.

Examine that question

exam BUSTERS

The following question tests your ability to select and explain relevant information.

Explain what dangers faced pioneers as they travelled to Oregon and California. (5 marks)

WARNING

THINK AHEAD: SELECT, PLAN, EXPLAIN

One of the biggest dangers that faced travellers was the weather. Heavy rainstorms on the Plains could turn the trail to mud and wagons could become stuck or damaged. Another danger that faced pioneers was …

Here are three steps to help you write your answer:

- In your exam you will only have a limited amount of time – so you cannot write about all the dangers! Choose more than one, but no more than three!
- Plan your answer before you begin to write.
- The key word in this question is **explain** – don't just write a list of the dangers, add an example to back up each point you make.

On the right is an answer that another candidate has started. Copy what they have written and complete the answer by explaining up to two more dangers.

Group 3: the gold miners

▼ **SOURCE 5** Newspaper headline about the discovery of gold in 1859

EL DORADO
OF THE
UNITED STATES OF AMERICA.

THE DISCOVERY
OF
INEXHAUSTIBLE GOLD MINES
IN
CALIFORNIA.

Tremendous Excitement among the Americans.

The Extensive Preparations
TO
MIGRATE TO THE GOLD REGION.
&c. &c. &c.

The great discovery of gold, in dust, scales and lumps, of quicksilver, platina, cinnabar, &c., &c., on the shores of the Pacific, has thrown the American people into a state of the wildest excitement. The intelligence from California, that gold can be picked up in lumps, weighing six or seven

▼ **SOURCE 6** The life of a gold miner

1 My name is Sam Bradley. I am a FORTY-NINER. My tale began in New York City in 1849. A friend read a newspaper story about a man called James Marshall who had found gold in a California ditch. It said that there was so much gold in California that the hills glistened in the setting sun!

2 I was poor and had a thirst for adventure. I decided to chance my luck and go there, even if it meant leaving my darling Janey; but I promised that I would be back with a gold ring just as soon as I had found my fortune.

3 Some folk paid to travel by boat to California, around South America. I couldn't afford a ticket, so I joined thousands of others on the California Trail. It was a difficult journey! It took months! As we crossed the Rockies, I teamed up with Jim Wheelihan from Vermont. We became partners.

4 We arrived in September 1849. Jim and I staked our CLAIMS near the Feather River Canyon, built a shelter and set to work with our washing pans in the river. We weren't alone. There were Americans, English, Scots, French, Germans and Italians. In the next valley there were Mexicans, Chinese and FREE BLACKS from the South. Most of us got on well enough.
We even made cradles to wash the dirt from the water. It was much easier than panning.

5 It was wet and filthy work. Jim and I found a few pieces of gold, but the wet diggings were soon used up. The next creek was so crowded that we could only claim a small area. That's where Jim accused me of panning his gold dust. He was right! He was spending so much time a-drinking and a-gambling, that somebody had to! He left and I fell ill ... that creek water never tasted like it should!

6 By 1852 most of the surface gold had gone and the mining companies moved in to get the gold from underground. I was taken on as a miner. It was dangerous and the pay was low. How I wished I was back in New York with my darling Janey!

7 At this time I saw my first hanging. Our miners' committee accused a Chinese miner of stealing someone else's claim, even though it had been empty for months! If only the committee could catch the big gangs! Those Chinese were treated badly. So were the Indians. With few women in the mining towns, many miners stole their wives. Some companies even used Indian children as slaves!

8 It's been eleven years since I left New York. I have heard a rumour that there is gold in Idaho, so that's where I'm heading for. Who knows, maybe I will be able to give that gold ring to my darling Janey after all ... if she'll have me!

■ DISCUSS

1 Study Source 5. How does the newspaper persuade people to emigrate (move) to California? Would it persuade you?

2 Work in pairs. You are both forty-niners (like Sam Bradley). One of you has enjoyed the experience of being a gold miner. The other has had a miserable time. Role-play a conversation between you.

⮂ SETTLER GRIDS

Use the information on these two pages to complete your Settler Grid on the gold miners.

2.3 *The Mormons: who made the biggest contribution, Joseph Smith or Brigham Young?*

Not all of the early settlers went to California and Oregon. In 1847 a religious group called the Mormons settled near the Great Salt Lake Valley. In this enquiry you will find out why they chose to live in such a lonely and BARREN place. For your final task you will compare the two Mormon leaders, Joseph Smith and Brigham Young and decide who you think made the biggest contribution to the Mormon movement and why.

▼ **SOURCE 1** A portrait of Joseph Smith

How successful was Joseph Smith as leader of the Mormons?

When the Mormon Church began in 1830, many Americans said that it would not last; but they had not counted on Joseph Smith, who started the Church.

Seven years earlier, in New York State, Joseph Smith claimed he had had a vision. He had been visited by an angel, who told him to dig up some gold plates on a hillside. Smith said the gold plates were like the pages of a book, each covered with ancient writing. He translated these plates and they became the Book of Mormon, the holy book of the Mormon Church. Smith chose several witnesses to write that they had seen the plates. He then returned the plates to the hillside.

Joseph Smith was a brilliant preacher. He told his followers to start building God's kingdom in America to prepare for the second coming of Christ. His ideas appealed to many people, but they upset many others. Wherever the Mormons went, it seemed they were not welcome.

◄ **SOURCE 2** A map to show the places from which the Mormons were forced to move, to avoid opposition

Factors explaining why the Mormons were unpopular in the East

IN KIRTLAND ———————→ **IN MISSOURI** ———————→ **IN NAUVOO**

1 Joseph Smith claimed to be a PROPHET. He told his followers that they were God's chosen people. Non-Mormons did not like this. They did not trust Smith.

2 The Mormons believed that hard work was good. They became very successful. Many were jealous of their success.

3 At Kirtland, Joseph Smith set up a bank for Mormons and non-Mormons. When the bank collapsed in 1837, many lost their savings. This made people think that Smith and the Mormons could not be trusted. The Mormons were chased out of Kirtland and moved to Missouri.

4 The Mormons were against slavery. This caused trouble when they settled in Missouri. Missouri was a slave owning state!

5 The Mormons were not unfriendly to the Indians. In Missouri, where many people were against the Indians, there was a rumour that the Mormons had asked the Indians to help them. The Mormons fled Missouri and settled in Nauvoo in Illinois.

6 At Nauvoo, Joseph Smith announced that men could marry more than one wife. You will remember that this is called polygamy. Non-Mormons were shocked. They thought that polygamy was a sin. They feared that it would lead to a Mormon population explosion.

In 1844 Joseph Smith was put in jail. A mob broke in and murdered him.

◄ **SOURCE 3** A cartoon from the 1840s commenting on polygamy

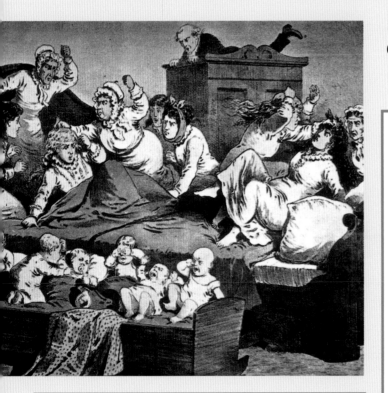

■ DISCUSS

1 What is happening in the cartoon in Source 3?
2 Is the cartoon for or against polygamy? Support your answer with details from the cartoon.

■ ACTIVITY

Look at the factors explaining why the Mormons were unpopular in the East. Your teacher can provide you with the factor cards.

1 In pairs, place the factors in order of importance.
2 List the most important reasons why the Mormons were unpopular in the East. Explain your choices.
3 How successful was Joseph Smith as leader of the Mormons? Copy and complete the table below to summarise Joseph Smith's leadership.

	Main strengths and achievements	**Main weaknesses and failures**
JOSEPH SMITH		

How successful was Brigham Young as leader of the Mormons?

Soon after Joseph Smith was killed, mobs attacked the homes of the Mormons in Nauvoo. Many Americans thought that this meant the end of the Mormon faith; but they had not counted on Brigham Young, the new leader.

Brigham Young decided that if the Mormons were to survive, they had to move west, to a place where they would be left alone. Young had read that the land around the Great Salt Lake Valley was the loneliest in North America. It sounded the ideal place to set up God's kingdom on earth. He persuaded his followers that the journey was worth making.

But the trip would be difficult. There were around 16,000 Mormons. The Great Salt Lake Valley was 2250 kilometres away from Nauvoo. There would be many dangers. Luckily, Brigham Young was a brilliant organiser. He had a plan!

▼ **SOURCE 4** Brigham Young

▼ **SOURCE 5** A map showing the journey to the Great Salt Lake Valley, 1846–1847

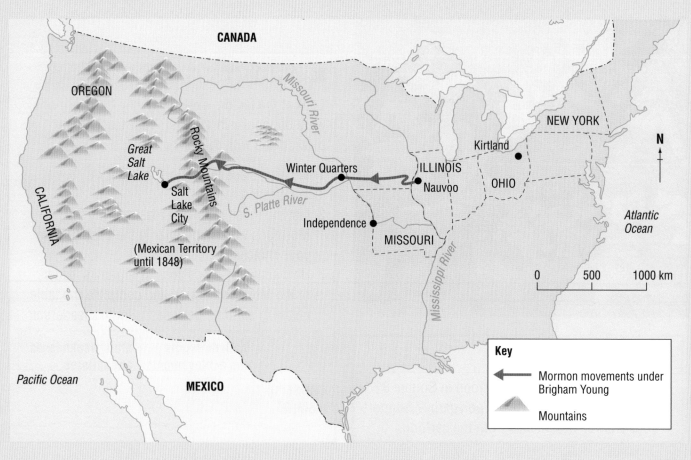

Brigham Young's plan – getting to the Great Salt Lake Valley

1 February 1846 – Take the Mormons out of Nauvoo.

2 Spring 1846 – I will lead an advance party. We will head as far west as possible. Every few miles we will build a rest camp for those who follow. We will plant crops and set up wagon workshops.

3 Summer 1846 – We will build a temporary settlement made of log cabins on the banks of the Missouri River. We will call this our Winter Quarters.

4 Autumn 1846 – The rest of our people will join us. We will spend the winter months at Winter Quarters.

5 Spring 1847 – I will lead a group to the Great Salt Lake Valley. I will choose the best place to build our holy city. The others will follow later.

Reminder!
Good discipline is important! We will sound a BUGLE to wake everyone for prayers at 5.00a.m. In case of Indian attack, the wagons will travel in double file and will park in a circular formation. A bugle will call us to prayer at 8.30p.m. Everyone needs to be asleep by 9.00p.m.

Unfortunately, not everything went to plan. At Winter Quarters, 700 Mormons died from starvation and disease. When Young reached the Great Salt Lake Valley in July 1847, he became ill with mountain fever. Even so, he was able to find enough strength to exclaim, 'This is the place!'

■ DISCUSS

What else would Brigham Young need to plan for the journey to the Great Salt Lake Valley? Discuss your ideas with a partner.

■ ACTIVITY

How successful was Brigham Young as leader of the Mormons?
   Copy and complete the table below to summarise Brigham Young's leadership so far. You will complete your table on page 37.

	Main strengths and achievements	Main weaknesses and failures
BRIGHAM YOUNG		

Building a new life

▲ **SOURCE 6** First reactions to the Mormons' new home

▼ **SOURCE 7** From the journal of William Clayton, one of the first Mormons to reach the Great Salt Lake Valley

There is an extensive, beautiful, level-looking valley from here to the lake. There is little timber in sight. There is no prospect of building log houses, but we can make Spanish bricks and dry them in the sun. For my own part I am happily disappointed in the appearance of the valley of the Great Salt Lake.

■ DISCUSS

Study Source 7. William Clayton said that he was 'happily disappointed' in the appearance of the Great Salt Lake Valley. What do you think he meant? Use Source 6 to help you decide.

Once Brigham Young reached the Great Salt Lake Valley, he faced a new set of problems.

Brigham Young's plan – living at the Great Salt Lake Valley

I will share the land fairly – each family will get a plot. The largest families will get the largest plots.

I will build an irrigation [water supply] system to provide everyone with fresh water.

I need skilled people. I will send MISSIONARIES to the east coast and Europe to persuade others to join the Mormons.

I will set up a fund – the PERPETUAL EMIGRATING FUND – to give money and equipment to people travelling to join us.

I will charge travellers who cross the Great Salt Lake Valley to help our funds.

Brigham Young kept the Mormon dream alive and his people remained loyal to him. However, he was not completely successful.

1 In 1848 the USA took the Great Salt Lake Valley from Mexico. Young asked the US government if he could create an independent Mormon state called Deseret, the 'Land of the honeybee'. The government refused and instead they made him governor of a smaller area – the Territory of Utah.

2 The Mormons were expected to obey US laws, but Young, with as many as 50 wives, was not keen to do this! Rumours began again. Travellers complained about the prices that the Mormons charged for supplies. When some Indians were converted to the Mormon faith, outsiders became suspicious.

3 In 1857 the President decided to replace Brigham Young as governor and sent 2,500 soldiers to Salt Lake City. Just when it seemed that a war was likely, the two sides reached a compromise. In 1858 the Mormons accepted a GENTILE governor. In return, the government allowed the Mormons to continue with their faith.

Brigham Young died in 1877. In 1896 the government finally allowed Utah to became a full member of the United States, but only after the Mormons had stopped practising polygamy.

■ ACTIVITY

Use the story of the Mormons in the Great Salt Lake Valley to complete your table from page 35, on the leadership of Brigham Young.

⇄ SETTLER GRIDS

Use the information on pages 32–37 to complete your Settler Grid on the Mormons.

This question is often asked in exams.

> Who made the biggest contribution to the Mormon movement, Joseph Smith or Brigham Young?
>
> (8 marks)

- This question asks you to compare the contributions of the two leaders. This means you should refer to *both leaders* in your answer.
- *Select evidence* from your notes on Joseph Smith and Brigham Young. Think about their strengths and weaknesses as leaders. Think about the different contributions that they made to the Mormon movement.
- You will have to *explain* which of the two leaders made the biggest contribution. You may decide that it was Joseph Smith, or Brigham Young, or you could argue that they both made equally important contributions to the Mormon movement! Whatever you decide, you must support your answer with *evidence* and *explanation*.

Here are three possible sentences to help start your answer:

> *I think Joseph Smith made a more important contribution to the Mormon movement than Brigham Young.*
>
> *I think Brigham Young made a more important contribution to the Mormon movement than Joseph Smith.*
>
> *I think that Joseph Smith and Brigham Young made equally important contributions to the Mormon movement.*

WARNING

DON'T FORGET TO USE EVIDENCE TO SUPPORT YOUR ARGUMENT

WARNING

REMEMBER TO COMPARE BOTH SIDES

Your teacher can provide you with a writing frame to help you complete your essay.

> *Useful connectives for comparing and contrasting*
>
> | *Comparing* | *Contrasting* |
> | --- | --- |
> | *equally* | *whereas/instead of* |
> | *in the same way* | *alternatively* |
> | *similarly/like* | *on the other hand/unlike* |

2.4 Staying there: why did homesteaders settle on the Plains?

Until the 1860s the Plains had been an area people went *through*. From the 1860s it became a place where people *settled*. That was a big change. You know all about the difficulties of living on the Plains from your work in Chapter 1. Over the next seven pages you will examine why, despite those difficulties, the Plains attracted homesteaders. You will learn about the problems they faced and how they survived. At the end you will create a memory map to sum up the main points.

HOMESTEADERS –
Farmers who
settled on the
Great Plains

▼ **SOURCE 1** An unidentified family of homesteaders, photographed outside their SOD HOUSE near West Union, Nebraska. In early photographs people had to keep still for much longer than we do today. It was very difficult to hold a smile for long enough!

■ DISCUSS

1 Study Source 1 carefully.
   a) What clothes are they wearing?
   b) How many children are there?
   c) What work might each member of the family do?
2 What sort of life do you think these people lead?

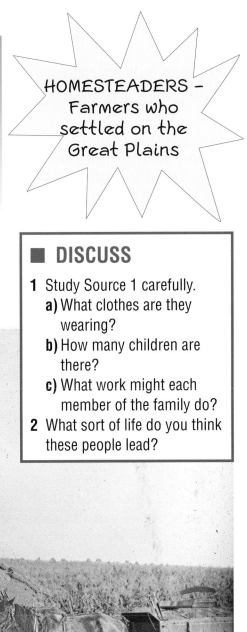

What attracted the homesteaders to the West?

There were three important PULL factors!

 The actions of the US government

The US government wanted settlers to move onto the Plains. In 1862 they passed the **Homestead Act**. This gave 160 acres of land to each family on the Plains. The land was free as long as the family farmed it and lived there for five years. In 1873 the US government passed the **Timber and Culture Act**. This awarded an extra 160 acres of land as long as 40 acres were planted with trees.

Millions of acres of free land became available as a result of these acts.

 The actions of the railroad companies

The government wanted to improve transport links across America. In 1862 two companies started building a TRANSCONTINENTAL railroad. Seven years later, the construction teams met in Utah and the railroad opened for traffic. It was not long before other railroads were being built across the Plains.

The railroad companies were given land by the US government. By advertising this land and selling it at low prices, the companies could pay the construction costs. As the companies sold more land, so more settlers used the railroads to get to the Plains.

PULL FACTOR 3 Letters

Letters home from those who had already settled on the Plains, and who were successfully farming, encouraged others to move west.

SETTLER GRIDS

Use the information on pages 39–41 to complete the first column of your Settler Grid on the homesteaders – **Reasons why they headed west**. Sort them into push and pull factors.

There were many PUSH factors that affected many different groups of people.

PUSH FACTORS FROM EUROPE

- There was a shortage of good farmland in Norway and Sweden.
- Unemployment and poverty affected many English, Germans, Irish, Russians and Scots.
- Jews and other religious groups wanted to escape from PERSECUTION at home.

PUSH FACTORS FROM THE EASTERN STATES

- There were shortages of farmland in the heavily populated Eastern states.
- There were few jobs for ex-soldiers after the AMERICAN CIVIL WAR.

PUSH FACTORS FROM THE SOUTHERN STATES

- Black Americans were still persecuted, even though they had been set free from slavery after the Civil War.
- Crops had failed and people were hungry.

■ ACTIVITY

Study Source 2. Explain what might have motivated these people to move onto the Great Plains. Consider both the **push** and **pull** factors.

▼ **SOURCE 2** The Shores family, who settled in Custer County, Nebraska, in 1887. Jerry Shores (far right) was a former slave

How did homesteaders survive on the Plains?

Prairie fire (out of control)

Swarm of grasshoppers eating crops

This buffalo dung burns too quickly on the stove. If only we had logs!

Sod house

More crops trampled by buffalo! We won't last another Nebraska winter!

Open, dried-up well

Dirt, fleas, and spiders ... Indians stole my washing!

Parched and withered maize

▲ SOURCE 3 A Nebraska homestead, summer 1869

▼ **SOURCE 4** Mrs O. C. Bell describes her experiences of homestead life in Nebraska in the 1880s

Still we ploughed and sowed and planted, tried to do our level best 'gainst hot winds, cyclones and hailstorms and every other doggone pest. Year by year we toiled and laboured, 'til we almost broke our backs. 'Half a crop' or 'total failure', scarce enough to pay the tax...

🔁 SETTLER GRIDS

1 Use Sources 3 and 4 to complete the second column of your Settler Grid on the homesteaders – **Problems that they faced**.

■ ACTIVITY

2 Compare Sources 3 and 5. Study the people, the animals and the landscape. Who or what is missing in Source 5?

3 What has changed?

■ DISCUSS

4 Work in pairs. Imagine you and your partner are elderly homesteaders, thinking back to the hardships of 1869. You must try to persuade your partner that you had the toughest time! Role-play your conversation using evidence to support your point of view.

▼ **SOURCE 5** A Nebraska homestead, summer 1889

■ **DISCUSS**

5 Look back to Chapter 1. Both the Plains Indians and the homesteaders had to solve the problems of living on the Plains. How and why were their solutions different?

6 Were there any problems that were not solved?

⤴ **SETTLER GRIDS**

7 Use Sources 3 and 5 to complete the third and fourth columns on the homesteaders – **Ways they solved their problems** and **How they affected the Indians**.

How important was the role of women in homesteading?

Homesteaders led a hard life on the Plains. It was important that everyone played a part. The men were responsible for building the home and farming, but what about the women? How important was their role?

▼ **SOURCE 6** Extracts from the diary of Luna E. Warner, aged fifteen, in 1871. The Warner family had just arrived in Kansas. They had a claim by the Solomon River so water was never a problem. At first they lived in a wooden cabin whilst they built their house

29 March *Our family went over to our claim and commenced to dig a cellar.*
6 April *Temperature at 98. We planted peas, turnips and squash on our claim.*
9 April *This morning we saw six buffaloes coming down the river. Louie took the rifle and I took the revolver. We lay down and waited until they got near; then Louie fired. How they ran!*
10 April *The snow fell into our faces all night. Our fireplace smokes very badly. It keeps our eyes crying all the time. The cabin is full of mice.*
14 April *Rainy. I dug fishworms and went fishing. There have been Indians seen in a good many places. We have to be very careful at night.*
18 April *The wind blew very hard. Everything out of doors blew away, even two pails of water.*
27 April *I killed three snakes today. Helped Papa plant onions and peas, sweet corn and melons.*
6 May *Uncle Howard and Henry worked our house. They raised the frame.*
10 May *We planted potatoes. Saw two beavers and a turkey gobbler.*
17 May *I am sixteen years old today. I do not feel so old.*

▼ **SOURCE 7** Extracts from the diary of Miriam Davis Colt in Kansas, 1856. The family had just arrived in Kansas. Their farm was not a success. They left before the end of the year

15 May *Have a fire out of doors to cook by … It is not very agreeable work, cooking out of doors in this windy, rainy weather, or when the scorching sun shines.*
26 May *Have been washing today, and dried our clothes right out in the burning hot sun. We do not leave them out on the dewy nights for fear of the Indians, who come thieving round, slying about, taking everything they can lay their hands on.*

- How many pupils were there in the school?
- How old do you think these pupils are?
- What problems might the teacher face in teaching this class?

▲ **SOURCE 8** A schoolteacher, or 'schoolmarm', with pupils, outside their school, Oklahoma, 1895. Most teachers on the Plains were young, unmarried women

▲ **SOURCE 9** A woman collecting cattle chips (dung) for fuel, Kansas, 1880s

■ **ACTIVITY**

Look at the information on these two pages and on pages 42–43. Think about the part played by women homesteaders.

1 Make a list of the jobs that women did.
2 Highlight any jobs that you think they shared with men. What jobs do you think were not shared?
3 Could the men have got on with their work without the women?
4 Which statement do you think best fits the role played by women in homesteading?
   a) Women had a vital role to play in homesteading.
   b) Women had an important role to play in homesteading.
   c) Women were not important in homesteading.

■ **DISCUSS**

Look back at your work on Plains Indian women in Chapter 1. Compare them with the women homesteaders.

1 How were the lives of these two groups of women similar?
2 How were they different?
3 Which way of life would you prefer?

How can a memory map save you time and help your memory?

smarter

REVISION

■ Memory maps help you link together important pieces of information. This is a good way of learning because it makes you think! You become actively involved in your revision. This is a lot better than simply reading through your folder hoping that you will remember what you have read. Your memory always works best when it has something active to do!

■ A memory map does not require lots of writing. You make your own images and use lots of colour instead. This helps you remember better.

■ Memory maps can be used in all sorts of different ways. They can be added to over time or built up over an enquiry. You can make a memory map before the exam, try to redraw it from memory, then add in what you have missed.

■ Making memory maps is fun!

How to build a memory map

Step 1 If you can, use a plain piece of A3 paper (landscape). You will need lots of space for your memory map. It should not look too busy or cramped.

Step 2 Draw the first draft of your map in pencil so that you can make any corrections that are needed.

Step 3 Start in the middle! Draw an image that sums up the topic for you in the centre of the page. Label your picture with the key title – **THE HOMESTEADERS**. PRINT the title of your main topic.

THE HOMESTEADERS

Step 4 Divide the topic into sub-topics – what are the main themes or ideas in the topic?

Step 5 Build out! Draw a line from the central image for your first sub-topic, rather like the large **bough** of a tree. Work in a clockwise direction, starting at 2 o'clock, and add the other boughs or sub-topics. Draw a simple image near each bough. Write the sub-topics on the boughs.

Use different colours for each bough. Use simple pictures, images and diagrams. Your memory map does not need to be an impressive work of art.

Step 6 Draw **branches** off each of the main boughs. Use the same colours as the boughs, but make the lines slightly thinner. On each branch write down key words connected to the sub-topic. Write these slightly smaller than the main theme.

Do not write sentences. Use **key words**. Ninety per cent of the words that students write down to revise are not needed for recall purposes!

Step 7 Sub-divide again and draw **twigs** on the branches of your memory map. Continue sub-dividing depending on how much detail you want to include. As you move further from the centre, the ideas become less important or central to the topic. You can show this by decreasing the size of the images as your memory map expands.

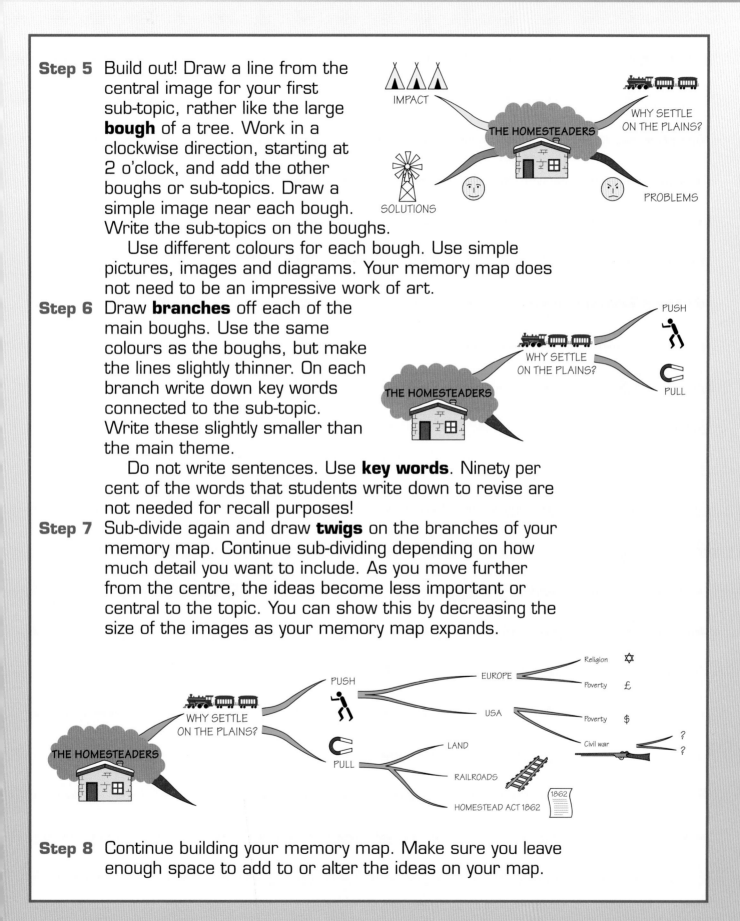

Step 8 Continue building your memory map. Make sure you leave enough space to add to or alter the ideas on your map.

2.5 *The cattlemen and cowboys*

RANCHERS –
People who own
(or manage) large
farms (ranches)
where cattle
are bred

While the homesteaders were settling on the Plains, much further to the south a different kind of farming was developing – the cattle industry. Over the next eight pages you will find out why it developed, and why the cattle ranchers ended up moving onto the Plains. For your final task you will compare different interpretations of COWBOYS.

How did the cattle industry develop? Part 1: the cattle drives from Texas

The Texas Longhorn was a tough beast! It could survive on the dry grasslands of Texas. Although its meat was not the best quality, it was good enough to sell and by the 1850s Texas was a major centre for cattle ranching.

Then came the American Civil War. Many Texans went to fight and the Longhorns were left to wander. By the end of the war the cattle herds were much bigger. This worried the ranchers. They realised that they could no longer sell all their beef to the people of Texas.

Cattle were not worth much unless they could be sold. The only way to do this was to drive the herds to wherever there was a demand for beef.

▼ **SOURCE 1** A map of the Plains showing the main cattle trails

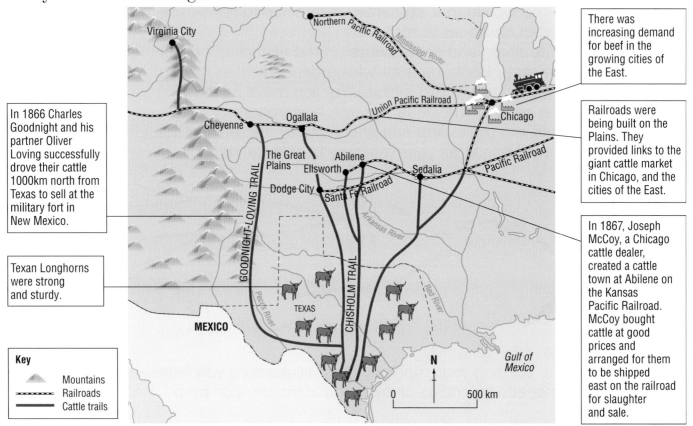

In 1866 Charles Goodnight and his partner Oliver Loving successfully drove their cattle 1000km north from Texas to sell at the military fort in New Mexico.

Texan Longhorns were strong and sturdy.

There was increasing demand for beef in the growing cities of the East.

Railroads were being built on the Plains. They provided links to the giant cattle market in Chicago, and the cities of the East.

In 1867, Joseph McCoy, a Chicago cattle dealer, created a cattle town at Abilene on the Kansas Pacific Railroad. McCoy bought cattle at good prices and arranged for them to be shipped east on the railroad for slaughter and sale.

Key

- Mountains
- Railroads
- Cattle trails

Charles Goodnight

I started my Texas cattle ranch in the 1850s. After the Civil War my partner Oliver Loving and I were the first to drive our cattle out of Texas to the North. Our route became known as the Goodnight–Loving Trail. Loving died in 1867 while fighting Comanche Indians.

Joseph McCoy

I am a Chicago cattle dealer. Abilene, my cow town, is in an ideal place. It lies on the route of the Kansas Pacific Railroad, which leads to Chicago. There is plenty of water and good grass. The town is near the end of the Chisholm Trail from Texas. I have employed engineers to extend the trail to Abilene by digging mounds of earth for the cattlemen to follow.

■ ACTIVITY

Why did Texas cattlemen drive their cattle north during the 1860s?

1 Make a set of five cards that explain why Texas cattlemen drove their cattle north during the 1860s. Use these headings:

- ■ The American Civil War
- ■ The growing cities in the East
- ■ The building of the railroads on the Plains
- ■ Charles Goodnight and Oliver Loving
- ■ Joseph McCoy

Summarise the information on your cards in bullet points. Your first card might look like this:

> The American Civil War 1862–1864
> - Many Texans fought in the American Civil War.
> - While they were away, the numbers of cattle increased.
> - When the war ended, there were too many cattle to sell in Texas for a profit.

2 Once you have made your cards, organise them into different types of causes to answer the question, e.g. economic causes (to do with money), technological causes, and causes to do with the role of individuals.

3 Are any of the causes connected? If so, how are they connected?

4 Are some causes more important than others, or are they all equally important? Is there a single cause that you think is the most important?

5 Copy the question onto a large sheet of paper. Arrange the cards on paper and stick them down. Now draw lines linking the cards to show the connections!

Cattle drive!

The aim of the game!

Play in pairs. You and your partner are rival Texas cattle drivers. You have to CATTLE DRIVE your herds of cattle from southern Texas to the cattle town of Abilene (look back to Source 1 on page 48). Your aims are to:

- reach Abilene before your rival
- try to get as many of your cattle to Abilene as you can.

To play

- Make your own counter. This could be a brand mark that you design yourself. See Source 2 for ideas.
- Each player starts with a herd of 3000 cattle.
- Take turns to throw a coin to move:
  Heads = move forward two places
  Tails = move forward one place
- After each turn note down what happens to you and record how many cattle you have left.

Your score

At the end count up how much money you made from the cattle drive. Multiply the price you receive for each cow at Abilene, by the number that reach their destination.

▶ **SOURCE 2**
A selection of cattle brands from the South-West, 1886

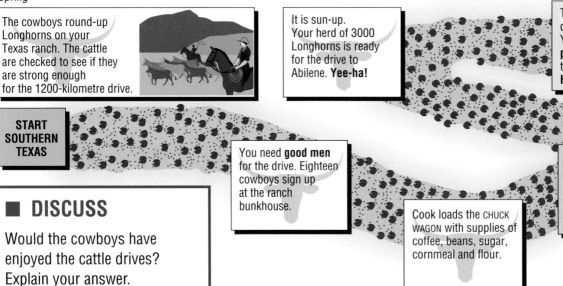

Spring

The cowboys round-up Longhorns on your Texas ranch. The cattle are checked to see if they are strong enough for the 1200-kilometre drive.

It is sun-up. Your herd of 3000 Longhorns is ready for the drive to Abilene. **Yee-ha!**

The Chisholm Trail is clearly marked. You make **good progress**. You cover twenty kilometres a day. **Have another go!**

START SOUTHERN TEXAS

You need **good men** for the drive. Eighteen cowboys sign up at the ranch bunkhouse.

Two cowboys are injured while branding a cow. They need treatment. **Miss a turn!**

Cook loads the CHUCK WAGON with supplies of coffee, beans, sugar, cornmeal and flour.

■ DISCUSS

Would the cowboys have enjoyed the cattle drives? Explain your answer.

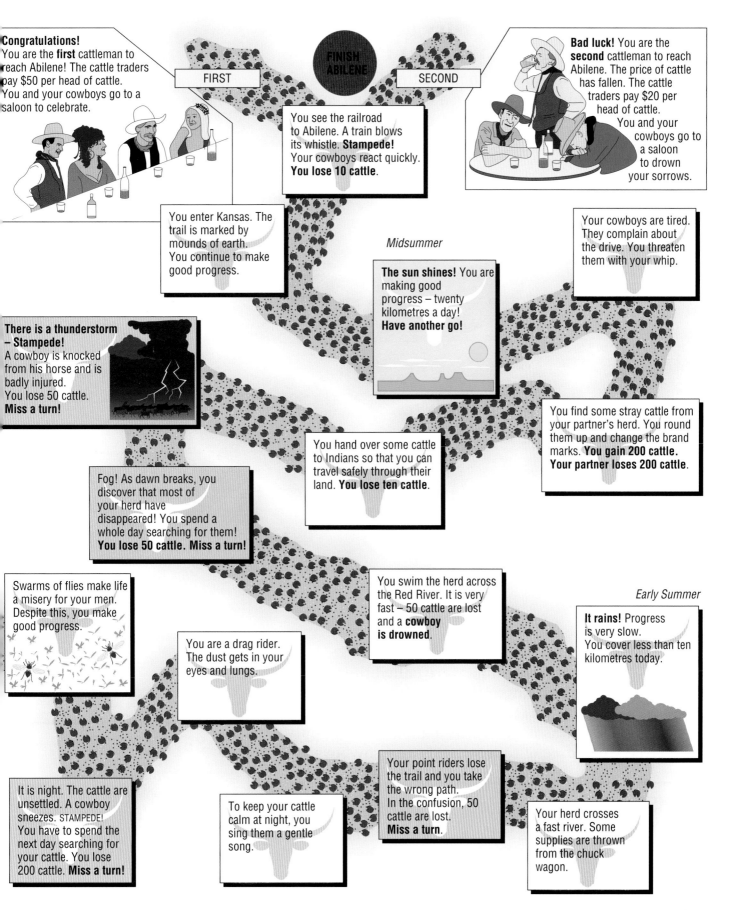

Congratulations!
You are the **first** cattleman to reach Abilene! The cattle traders pay $50 per head of cattle. You and your cowboys go to a saloon to celebrate.

FIRST

FINISH ABILENE

SECOND

Bad luck! You are the **second** cattleman to reach Abilene. The price of cattle has fallen. The cattle traders pay $20 per head of cattle. You and your cowboys go to a saloon to drown your sorrows.

You see the railroad to Abilene. A train blows its whistle. **Stampede!** Your cowboys react quickly. **You lose 10 cattle**.

You enter Kansas. The trail is marked by mounds of earth. You continue to make good progress.

Your cowboys are tired. They complain about the drive. You threaten them with your whip.

Midsummer

The sun shines! You are making good progress – twenty kilometres a day! **Have another go!**

There is a thunderstorm – Stampede!
A cowboy is knocked from his horse and is badly injured. You lose 50 cattle. **Miss a turn!**

You find some stray cattle from your partner's herd. You round them up and change the brand marks. **You gain 200 cattle. Your partner loses 200 cattle**.

You hand over some cattle to Indians so that you can travel safely through their land. **You lose ten cattle**.

Fog! As dawn breaks, you discover that most of your herd have disappeared! You spend a whole day searching for them! **You lose 50 cattle. Miss a turn!**

You swim the herd across the Red River. It is very fast – 50 cattle are lost and a **cowboy is drowned**.

Early Summer

It rains! Progress is very slow. You cover less than ten kilometres today.

Swarms of flies make life a misery for your men. Despite this, you make good progress.

You are a drag rider. The dust gets in your eyes and lungs.

It is night. The cattle are unsettled. A cowboy sneezes. STAMPEDE! You have to spend the next day searching for your cattle. You lose 200 cattle. **Miss a turn!**

To keep your cattle calm at night, you sing them a gentle song.

Your point riders lose the trail and you take the wrong path. In the confusion, 50 cattle are lost. **Miss a turn**.

Your herd crosses a fast river. Some supplies are thrown from the chuck wagon.

How did the cattle industry develop? Part 2: ranching on the Great Plains

By the 1870s, ranchers began to move their cattle herds onto the Great Plains. There were a number of reasons for this.

> The northern plains are empty! There are very few homesteaders there. The Indians have moved onto RESERVATIONS. Hunters have shot many buffalo. The grass is good and there is plenty of it.

> Driving cattle from Texas has become more and more difficult. Homesteaders have started to build their farms across the routes of the cattle trails!

> The TRANSCONTINENTAL railroad crosses the northern plains. This makes it easier to send my cattle to market.

> A famous rancher called John Iliffe has proved that cattle can survive the long winters on the Great Plains. He has sold beef to railroad builders and to the Sioux Indians on their reservations.

> The cold winters of the northern plains kill the disease-carrying ticks that affect my cattle. With healthier cattle I can breed Texas Longhorns with other, fatter breeds.

The open range

Ranches on the northern plains were called the 'OPEN RANGE'. The term 'open range' described the vast area of unfenced land that was claimed by the ranch owner for his cattle. All that was needed was a good water supply and a large workforce of ranch-hands and cowboys.

■ DISCUSS

Can you think of any problems that might face the cattle ranchers once they moved onto the Plains? Discuss what these might be with a partner.

⮂ SETTLER GRIDS

Use the information on pages 48–52 to complete the first column of your Settler Grid on the cattlemen and cowboys – **Reasons why they headed West**.

How did the cattle industry develop? Part 3: the end of the open range

The early 1880s was a boom time for cattle ranching and huge profits were made. However, as more ranchers moved in to take more land, others began to worry about the future.

SETTLER GRIDS

Use the information on this page to complete the second column of your Settler Grid on the cattlemen and cowboys – **Problems that they faced**.

Overgrazing: By 1883, so many cattle were grazing on the plains that the grass could not grow properly.

Drought: During the summer of 1883, there was a drought. The grass became very dry and many cattle went hungry.

Falling beef prices: At the same time, the price of beef began to fall. Ranchers decided to keep their cattle on the open range rather than take them to market. This made the problem of overgrazing even worse. More cattle became thin and weak.

The winter of 1886–1887: The awful winter killed thousands of weakened cattle. Many ranchers lost their herds and went out of business.

Barbed wire fences:

Unemployment: The smaller ranches required fewer cowboys. Many lost their jobs. The days of the open range were over!

After the winter, the open range was divided into smaller ranches, each with fewer cattle. Barbed wire, which was cheap and strong, was used to fence the land. Fences made it easier for ranchers to manage their herds.

Wind pumps: Wind pumps were used to supply water. Now the cattle could be kept anywhere on the plains.

Who were the cowboys?

The word 'cowboy' was used to describe the men who worked on the cattle drives and ranches. Many had left the southern states at the end of the Civil War and they included large numbers of black Americans and Mexicans. They worked out of doors in all weathers. They led a difficult life and they were poorly paid.

The work of the cowboy

CATTLE BRANDING: As there were no fences, cattle had to be clearly identified. The cowboys applied the ranch brand mark to young cattle.

Round up: Cowboys rounded up the cattle in the spring and summer. They drove the cattle to the nearest railroad for sale.

Line riding: The cowboys kept watch over the ranch boundary. They herded stray cattle back onto the ranch and sometimes had to deal with cattle RUSTLERS and wild animals.

Stetson

Bandana

Boots

Spurs

Saddle

Slicker coat

Leather gloves

Six-shooter

Leather chaps

Lariat

■ ACTIVITY

This cowboy needs to get ready for another day's work! Your teacher will give you an outline copy of the cowboy.

1 Draw arrows to connect the items of clothing and equipment to where they would be worn by the cowboy, or carried on his horse.
2 Explain what each item of clothing or equipment was used for.

🔁 SETTLER GRIDS

3 Use the information on this page to complete the next part of your Settler Grid on the cattlemen and the cowboys – **Ways they solved their problems**.

By the time that cattle ranching had moved onto the Plains, most of the Indian tribes were living on reservations. You will learn about these reservations in Chapter 4.

What were the cowboys like?

What were the real cowboys like? Were they ordinary, hard working men or the lowest of the low? Or were they the romantic heroes of the Hollywood Western films?

▲ **SOURCE 3** *In Without Knocking!* by Charles Russell, the 'cowboy artist'. Russell worked on cattle ranches between 1890 and 1892

■ **ACTIVITY**

Do you think cowboys were heroes or villains?

4 Look at Source 3. What is happening? What impression of the cowboys does this source give?

5 On your own copy of Sources 4–6 use a colour to highlight the words and phrases that describe the cowboys as heroes. Use another colour to highlight the words and phrases that describe the cowboys as villains.

6 Use the sources and the information on pages 54–55 to explain whether you think the cowboys were heroes or villains. Remember to back up your point of view with evidence and explanation.

▼ **SOURCE 4** John Baumann writing in the *Fortnightly Review*, 1 April 1887

He [the cowboy] is on the whole a loyal, hard working fellow, grit to the backbone and tough as whipcord …

▼ **SOURCE 5** Extract from the *Topeka Commonwealth* (Kansas), 15 August 1871

He [the cowboy] generally wears a revolver [six-shooter] on each side, which he will use with as little hesitation on a man as a wild animal. Such a character is dangerous and desperate and each one has generally killed a man.

▼ **SOURCE 6** Part of the poem *Texas Types – the Cowboy*, written by Larry Chittenden, a New York journalist who took up ranching in Texas in 1883

*He wears a big hat and big spurs and all
   that
And leggins of fancy fringed leather;
He takes pride in his boots and the pistol
   he shoots
And he's happy in all kinds of weather.*

*He can sing, he can cook, yet his eyes
   have the look
Of a man that to fear is a stranger;
Yes, his cool, quiet nerve will always
   subserve [help]
In his wild life of duty and danger.*

*He is loyal as steel, but demands a square
   deal [fair wage],
And he hates and despises a coward.
Yet the cowboy you'll find unto woman is
   kind,
Though he'll fight till by death
   overpowered.*

2.6 *Who had the most impact on the Plains Indians?*

Over the last 32 pages you have been working on your Settler Grids, comparing the different groups of settlers. Now you have an important review task: to decide which group had the most impact on the lives of the Plains Indians.

■ DISCUSS

Study Source 1 carefully.

1 Where was the highest density of towns with over 5000 inhabitants by 1895?
2 Think back to your work on the homesteaders and cattle ranchers. Why do you think that most of the large towns in Source 1 were in this part of the USA?

▼ **SOURCE 1** North America in 1895, showing the expansion of the United States

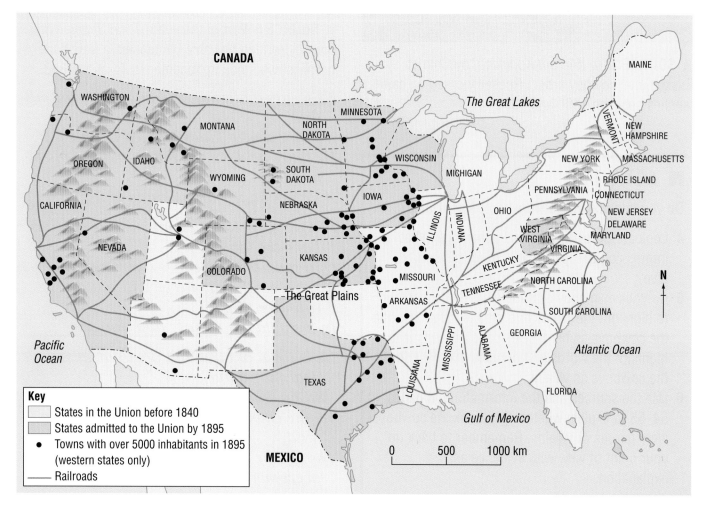

Key
- States in the Union before 1840
- States admitted to the Union by 1895
- • Towns with over 5000 inhabitants in 1895 (western states only)
- — Railroads

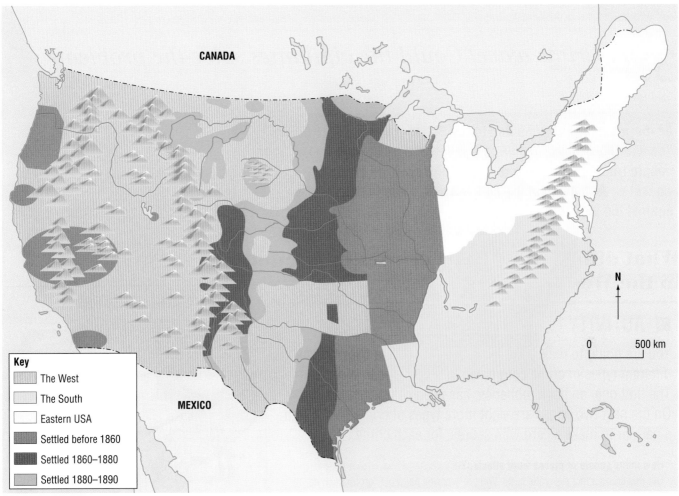

Key
- The West
- The South
- Eastern USA
- Settled before 1860
- Settled 1860–1880
- Settled 1880–1890

▲ **SOURCE 2** Map showing the areas of settlement in the USA by 1890

⮂ SETTLER GRIDS

3 What impact did each group of settlers have on the Indians? Copy the list of settlers shown below. Use the notes on your Settler Grids and Sources 1 and 2 to summarise how they affected the Indians.

- The mountain men
- The pioneers
- The gold miners
- The Mormons
- The homesteaders
- The cattlemen and cowboys

4 Now think about how much impact each group had on the Indians. You can use this colour code for each group:

Green – had very little impact on the Plains Indians
Amber – had some impact on the Plains Indians
Red – had a big impact on the lives of the Plains Indians.

■ ACTIVITY

5 Look at Source 2. Compare this to Source 4 on page 6. During which part of the nineteenth century did the settlers begin to make the biggest impact on the Indians?

6 Why do you think that some parts of the USA were still unsettled by the end of the nineteenth century?

CHAPTER 3 *Law and order*

3.1 *Crime wave! Could the vigilantes solve the problem?*

As more people moved out onto the Plains the crime rate grew. You will find out why the West was lawless and how some ordinary people tried to solve the problem themselves by becoming VIGILANTES. At the end of the unit you will argue the case for or against the vigilantes.

What different types of crimes happened in the West?

■ ACTIVITY

You are going to make a set of Top Trumps cards based on the different types of crime committed in the American West.
The first one, on bank robberies, has been completed for you.
On the next two pages are eight more types of crime. Work with a partner to make a card with scores, for each crime.

How many people or places were affected?
Did this crime affect everyone in the West or just one particular group such as homesteaders?
On this card just people living in towns were affected so we have awarded it 6/10.

How serious was the crime?
How serious do you think this crime was? Think about whether people were killed or not and how people were punished for committing this crime. The more serious the crime the higher the score you give it.
On this card most bank robberies did not involve deaths so we have awarded it 7/10.

Famous gangs or gunfighters
Were there famous gangs or gunfighters associated with this crime?
In this case there was the James Gang so we have awarded it 9/10.

Most important factor which explains this crime
This is left blank at the moment. You will use it later to improve your game.

BANK ROBBERIES

How many people or places were affected?	6/10
How serious was the crime?	7/10
Famous gangs or gunfighters	9/10
Most important factor which explains this crime	/10

When your card set is complete use it to play a game of Top Trumps with your partner. You might swap with another pair. The winner is the person who wins the whole set of cards.

Bank robberies

As towns grew banks were set up. These held the townspeople's cash. With few or no lawmen in the towns these banks were an easy target for outlaws. Gangs, like the James Gang, could ride in, steal the money and disappear before any resistance could be organised.

Claim jumping

CLAIM JUMPING was a problem that affected just miners in the mining towns. There were no forces of law and order in these new towns so latecomers could use violence to steal the valuable claims of others. Miners were physically attacked and in extreme cases murdered.

Fence cutting

Fence cutting took place out on the open range in the 1880s and 1890s. The CATTLE BARONS were trying to fence in large areas with barbed wire. They wanted to control access to water by fencing it off. Many small ranchers and homesteaders resisted this by cutting the wire fences.

Cattle rustling

Rustling was a problem for ranchers on the open range because their cattle roamed freely. This made them an easy target for rustlers – people who steal cattle. Branding the cattle made this more difficult. But rustlers could change the brand before selling the cattle or adding them to their own herd. Rustling was one of the problems that led to the 'Johnson County War' (see page 66).

Horse stealing

With so many horses in the West, horse stealing was a common crime. Horses were both very valuable and essential to life on the Plains. Horse stealing was regarded as a dishonourable crime and was treated very seriously. Horse thieves were often hanged. In contrast, for the Plains Indians horse stealing was an essential part of their way of life. It was one way in which a warrior gained honour and wealth.

Racial attacks

Thousands of Chinese emigrated to the United States. Many went to help build the railroads. Those that settled in mining and cow towns were often the victims of racial attacks. The worst case was in Rock Springs in Wyoming where 51 Chinese people were killed in a riot in 1885. Other groups in the West who suffered racial attack were black Americans, Indians and Mexicans.

Shootings

Some historians estimate that as many as 20,000 people were shot dead in the West during the years 1866–1900. Other historians disagree. One historian who studied violence in the cow towns claimed that only 45 people were shot dead during the years 1867–1885. Men like Billy the Kid gained a reputation as ace gun fighters.

Stagecoach robbery

Stagecoaches could be stopped far away from towns and robbed of any money they or their passengers were carrying. The single, armed guard employed by stagecoach companies could not fight off a large armed gang. One famous outlaw, Black Bart, robbed 27 Wells–Fargo stagecoaches before he was caught.

Train robbery

The first train robbery took place in 1866. From then on gangs like Butch Cassidy and the Wild Bunch regularly stopped trains to steal the money they carried. Far away from the nearest towns and any forces of law and order the trains made an easy target. This remained a very frequent crime until 1900.

What reasons were there to explain the crimes?

Who's in charge?
The new cow towns and mining towns grew very quickly. At first there was no organised government so there was no law enforcement. National politicians were not keen to spend much money in an area with so few voters. When trouble started there was no one to stop the violence.

Wild young men
At the same time these towns were full of young men, cowboys and miners, with money to spend on having a good time, and those people who made a living from them like saloon bar owners, gamblers and prostitutes.

Ethnic divisions
In the West there were different ethnic groups mixed together who might easily come into conflict. There were black Americans, Chinese, Europeans, Indians, Mexicans and Easterners.

Old grudges
Amongst the Easterners were many ex-soldiers from the Civil War, Unionists and Confederates, who were unwilling to forgive and forget the War. Trouble could and did break out between these different groups.

Such a big country!
The West was a vast area and transport was slow. This made it difficult to enforce law and order. OUTLAWS could disappear before the forces of law and order arrived.

Thirst for wealth
The West was full of different groups of people competing for land and wealth. There were cowboys and townspeople, homesteaders and ranchers, big ranchers and small ranchers. Trouble could easily break out between them and often did.

'A man's got to do what a man's got to do'
The West was dominated by a basic code of honour, the 'Code of the West'. If you had a problem you sorted it out yourself. As everyone carried guns, disputes often ended in a shooting. If you killed someone in self-defence you had not broken the law.

■ ACTIVITY

1 There were seven factors about the West that led to the crime problem. They are shown on the left. Put each factor into one of the following five categories:

■ Geographical: concerning the environment of the West
■ Cultural: concerning the way of life in the West
■ Political: concerning who was in charge in the West
■ Economic: concerning how much money people had in the West
■ Social: concerning how different groups lived together in the West

2 Look back at your Top Trumps cards. Which factor do you think best explains the reasons for each crime?

3 Using the following ratings add a score for the last row to complete your Top Trumps cards:

Geographical: 5
Cultural: 4   Political: 3
Economic: 2   Social: 1

For example, if you think that the most important factor which led to bank robberies is explained in 'Who's in charge?' then you would add 3 points to your card, as this is a political factor.

How did the US government attempt to solve the problem of crime?

As the West was settled, towns grew and local government developed. To begin with, areas of the West were organised as territories. Eventually these became states of the United States of America. Within these territories and states there were a range of people and forces responsible for keeping law and order. All of these worked within the law, but their small numbers and the vast area of the West made it very difficult for them to be effective.

■ **DISCUSS**

1 Look back to the different types of crime on pages 59–60. Which one of the law enforcers below would deal with each of the crimes?
2 How do you think the different types of crime would have been punished?

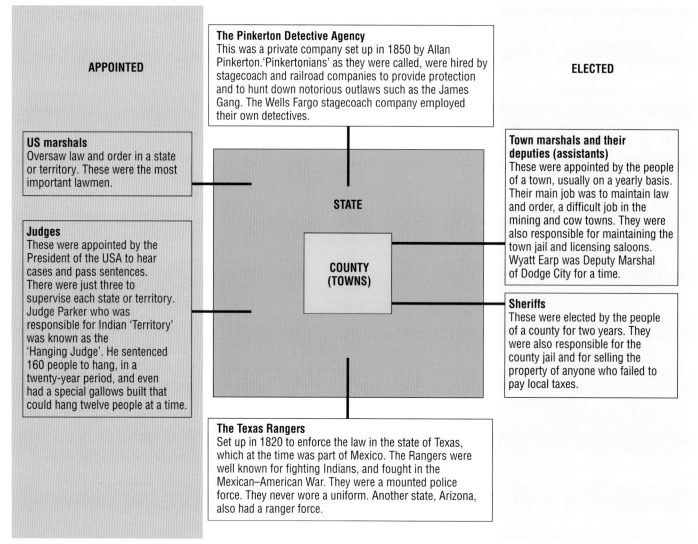

APPOINTED

ELECTED

The Pinkerton Detective Agency
This was a private company set up in 1850 by Allan Pinkerton. 'Pinkertonians' as they were called, were hired by stagecoach and railroad companies to provide protection and to hunt down notorious outlaws such as the James Gang. The Wells Fargo stagecoach company employed their own detectives.

US marshals
Oversaw law and order in a state or territory. These were the most important lawmen.

Judges
These were appointed by the President of the USA to hear cases and pass sentences. There were just three to supervise each state or territory. Judge Parker who was responsible for Indian 'Territory' was known as the 'Hanging Judge'. He sentenced 160 people to hang, in a twenty-year period, and even had a special gallows built that could hang twelve people at a time.

STATE

COUNTY (TOWNS)

Town marshals and their deputies (assistants)
These were appointed by the people of a town, usually on a yearly basis. Their main job was to maintain law and order, a difficult job in the mining and cow towns. They were also responsible for maintaining the town jail and licensing saloons. Wyatt Earp was Deputy Marshal of Dodge City for a time.

Sheriffs
These were elected by the people of a county for two years. They were also responsible for the county jail and for selling the property of anyone who failed to pay local taxes.

The Texas Rangers
Set up in 1820 to enforce the law in the state of Texas, which at the time was part of Mexico. The Rangers were well known for fighting Indians, and fought in the Mexican–American War. They were a mounted police force. They never wore a uniform. Another state, Arizona, also had a ranger force.

The systems set up by the US government to keep law and order did not always work. In some places there were not enough lawmen and not all of them were honest. Sometimes this led the people of the West to take the law into their own hands.

▲ **SOURCE 1** The structure of law and order

How did the vigilantes try to solve the problem of crime?

There were over 200 vigilante groups recorded west of the Mississippi. But their actions were not always just. In Downieville, California, in 1851, vigilantes LYNCHED a Mexican woman who had killed a drunken miner who had attacked her. A newspaper at the time commented, 'Had this woman been an American instead of a Mexican, instead of being hung for the deed, she would have been praised for it. It was not her guilt that condemned the unfortunate woman, but her Mexican blood.'

▼ **SOURCE 2** Professor T. J. Dimsdale, writing in *The Vigilantes of Montana*, 1866

Such was the lawless state of affairs that five men in Virginia City and four in Bannack started the Montana Vigilantes. In a few weeks it was known that the voice of justice had spoken. The vigilantes struck from his hand the weapon of the murderer, warned the thief to steal no more and forced the ruffians, who had so long maintained a reign of terror in Montana, to flee the territory.

▼ **SOURCE 3** Edward Buffem, a journalist working as a miner, witnessed vigilantes in action. Two Frenchmen and one Chilean, none of whom could speak English, had been accused of committing a murder three months earlier. A miners' court of about 200 men had condemned them to death

Vainly they called for an interpreter, for their cries were drowned by the now infuriated mob. The wagon was drawn from under them, and they were launched into eternity.

▼ **SOURCE 4** The editor of the *Idaho World*, printed on 2 September 1865

A general lawlessness prevails through all these territories of Montana, Idaho, Colorado and Utah resolving itself in the form of these vigilante committees. Everywhere they have brought trouble upon the community. The remedy for the existing evils is greater than the evils.

■ ACTIVITY

Your task is to decide whether vigilantes were a force for good or evil in the West. Your teacher can give you copies of Sources 2–5 to help you.

1 Study Source 2. Professor Dimsdale is in favour of the vigilantes. Highlight the words or phrases he uses to describe what life was like before the Montana Vigilantes were started. What crimes were the Montana Vigilantes concerned about?

2 Study Source 3. Edward Buffem was against the vigilantes. What one collective noun makes his opinion obvious?

3 Study Sources 4 and 5 and decide which is for vigilantes and which is against.

4 Now come to a conclusion about the vigilantes: did they make the crime situation better or worse? Why is it difficult to decide?

▼ **SOURCE 5** The report in a Denver newspaper on a vigilante hanging in 1879

The hanging was not only well deserved but a positive gain to the country, saving it at least five or six thousand dollars.

3.2 *Would you pardon Billy the Kid?*

One famous outlaw was William H. Bonney, alias Billy the Kid. Many books have been written about him and his life has inspired more than 40 films. In February 2001 his descendants asked if he could receive a posthumous (after death) pardon for his crimes. Would you pardon him? Study the evidence and decide.

■ **DISCUSS**

Read the box below entitled 'Billy the Kid: the facts'. Do you think he sounds like a hero or a villain?

▼ **SOURCE 1** A tintype (an early type of photograph) of Billy taken at Fort Sumner, New Mexico in 1880. Tintypes are reversed images, so you often see this one printed back to front. This has confused many people into thinking that Billy was left-handed. One Hollywood film version of his life was even called *The Left Handed Gun*!

BILLY THE KID: THE FACTS

- Born in the eastern USA around 1859 and moved to New Mexico with his mother and brother some time in the 1870s.
- Got into trouble as a teenager and was jailed for theft.
- In 1877 he killed a man.
- July 1878 — he gained a reputation as a top gunfighter during the LINCOLN COUNTY WAR.
- Arrested on 23 December 1880, and later tried and sentenced to hang for his part in the murder of Sheriff William Brady of Lincoln.
- Killed two deputies while escaping from Lincoln County Jail, April 1881.
- Forced to live as an outlaw when the Governor of New Mexico failed to grant Billy the pardon he had been promised.
- Acted as a champion of the downtrodden Mexicans in New Mexico, a bit like Robin Hood.
- Tracked down and shot dead by Sheriff Pat Garrett at Fort Sumner, New Mexico on 15 July 1881.

BILLY THE KID: THE EVIDENCE

▼ **SOURCE 2** These interviews have been taken from *American Life Histories: Manuscripts from the Federal Writers' Project, 1936–1940*, an oral history project. Each of the people below was interviewed about their experiences living in New Mexico at the same time as Billy the Kid. You can visit the website to find some more interviews at: http://memory.loc.gov/ammem/wpaquery.html

Interviewee 1 – Louis Bousman, aged 76 years
Billy was fourteen when he killed his first man in Silver City, New Mexico. He was a porter and bootblack [shoe polisher] around the hotel. He came from New York, or somewhere in the East. There was a fellow in the hotel who kept bullying Billy, and Billy told him that if he did not let him alone he would kill him. The next morning the fellow started bullying Billy again, and grabbed a hold of him, so Billy killed him. Then he stole a horse and left, and went down on the Pecos River where Chisholm's ranch was, and joined as a cowboy.

Interviewee 2 – Lorencita Miranda, aged 68 years
My husband and I were living on our farm just above Lincoln during the Lincoln County War . . . I remember the day the McSween home was burned. We could see the flames and smoke, but we stayed at home for we were scared to death to stick our heads out of the house. Billy the Kid came to our house several times and drank coffee with us. We liked him for he was always nice to the Spanish people...

Interviewee 3 – Amelia Church, aged 68 years
I remember all the facts about that escape. Billy the Kid was playing cards with Bell, while Ollinger, his other guard, was at dinner across the street, he [Billy] saw his chance and grabbed Bell's gun. Bell darted down the inside stairway, but Billy the Kid was too quick for him, he fired and Bell fell dead at the bottom of the stairs. Billy the Kid then walked calmly to a window and shot Ollinger down as he came running when he heard the shooting. The 'Kid' then threw the gun on Ollinger who lay dying...

Interviewee 4 – Charles Ballard, aged 61 years
I remember good times I had with Billy the Kid. He was not an outlaw in manners – was quiet, but good company . . . That was why he had so many friends. We often raced horses together. He was a fine rider. Billy was credited with more killings than he ever did. However, there were plenty that could be counted against him.

Interviewee 5 – George Bede, aged 61 years
During the time I was growing up, I often met the Kid and heard father and the other cowhands talking about him. Whenever I met him he acted mighty decent and it was generally said that he never turned a fellow down that was up against it and called for a little help. But also, the folks said he would shoot a man just to see the fellow give the dying kick. It was said he got a powerful lot of amusement out of watching a fellow, that he didn't like, twist and groan.

■ ACTIVITY

1 Study each interviewee's account. Copy and complete the table below to summarise their opinions of Billy. Then complete the third column to record whether or not their account makes you think Billy deserves a pardon. The first row has been done for you.

Interviewee	Overall view of Billy	Does Billy deserve a pardon?
Louis Bousman	Billy was standing up for himself and had warned the man not to continue bullying him. He killed only one man, on a matter of pride, and then began working as a cowboy.	Yes
Lorencita Miranda		
Amelia Church		
Charles Ballard		
George Bede		

2 Use your work on pages 64–65 to decide whether or not Billy the Kid should be pardoned.

3.3 'The Johnson County War' – was the West in chaos or were the forces of law and order in control?

Sometimes crime got so bad it seemed more like a war. On this spread you will find out about the so-called 'Johnson County War' – and write a news feature to tell your readers what is going on there.

■ ACTIVITY

You are a reporter for the *Chicago Herald*. You have been sent to report on the Johnson County War. You have to send your script by telegraph so it must be short. You must include:

■ A brief description of what happened and an explanation of why it happened. Maximum of 200 words.

■ Quotes from one or two of the people who were there – a 'Regulator', the Sheriff of Buffalo or one of the US cavalry. Maximum of 20 words for each quote. You will have to invent these.

■ Your newspaper can't decide how to interpret the Johnson County War so they want you to write two possible conclusions. One should argue that the Johnson County War shows that the West is in chaos and under the rule of thugs and gangs of hired killers. The other should show how effectively the forces of law and order worked to avoid a bloodbath. Maximum of 75 words for each conclusion.

The background – 1870s

Cattle ranching came to Johnson County in the 1870s. Cattle barons set up huge ranches. They each had thousands of cattle. They formed the Wyoming Stock Growers Association which met in Cheyenne. Important politicians, like the state governor, were members. They became very powerful. The Association protected the interests of its members.

Tension grows – 1880s

In the 1880s the cattle barons had problems.

Cattle ranching on the open range is in trouble – because of overgrazing, drought and falling beef prices (see page 53 to find out more).

Small ranchers and homesteaders have settled in Johnson County on our land. We have put up fences, and we have blocked their access to streams and rivers but still they keep coming.

And they rustle our cattle. They round up our calves before they're branded. We take them to court, but the JURIES are all local men in Johnson County. They won't convict. What can we do? We have blacklisted the men on the juries – they'll never work for one of us again. And we have had a few of them killed by hired guns. They got what they deserved.
But...

The flashpoint – 1892

In 1892 the smaller ranchers planned a combined round-up of cattle on the open range. The cattle barons believed that more of their cattle would be rustled. So they planned a decisive, armed invasion of Johnson County.

The cattle barons:

✔ got the support of local politicians for their invasion
✔ were supplied a case of guns by the acting governor
✔ hired 24 gunfighters from Texas on $5 a day plus expenses with a $50 bonus for each dead 'rustler'
✔ allegedly drew up a death list of 70 names
✔ were supplied a special train by the Union Pacific Railroad Company to bring the invasion force of cattlemen and gunfighters to Wyoming
✔ brought in reporters from the *Cheyenne Sun* and the *Chicago Herald* to report on what they were doing
✔ named themselves 'The Regulators'.

The 'War' – 1892

▼ **SOURCE 1** 'The Regulators' photographed in custody at Fort D A Russell, 4 May 1892

1 The Regulators first cut the telegraph wires to Johnson County.
2 Then they headed for Buffalo. On the way they attacked the KC ranch where they captured two visiting fur trappers and killed Nick Ray.
3 Nate Champion held them off all day until they burnt him out of his cabin.
4 Meanwhile, the Regulators had been spotted and the alarm was raised in Buffalo. The Sheriff of Buffalo gathered a large force of local men to stop them.
5 The invaders retreated to the TA ranch. Here the Sheriff and his men surrounded them.
6 One invader escaped to get help and the cattle barons persuaded the US cavalry to rescue them.
7 At the TA ranch, the cavalry persuaded the local men to stop shooting and then arrested the Regulators.
8 For their own safety they put the Regulators in prison well away from Johnson County.

The trial

• The Regulators were put on trial but the cattle barons used their influence to get the court case moved to Cheyenne.
• The residents of Johnson County were charged with the cost of feeding and housing the prisoners. Johnson County ran out of money.
• The trappers who witnessed the murders of Nick Ray and Nate Champion disappeared!
• The case was dropped. The Regulators went free.

The consequences

The 'War' marked the end of the open range in Johnson County. The cattle barons got a lot of bad publicity. Their Association closed down in Cheyenne. Their influence on local affairs decreased. The smaller ranchers were able to get on with their lives.

CHAPTER 4 *Why was there conflict on the Plains?*

4.1 *Why did war break out on the Plains?*

When outsiders and Indians first met on the Plains, relations between them were generally friendly. However, once ranchers and homesteaders began to settle on the Plains there was trouble. On the next four pages you will get an overview of the whole period and consider the strengths and weaknesses of the US army.

■ ACTIVITY

The diagram on the right shows a cycle of events that was repeated again and again from the 1850s onwards.

On your own copy include an example in each box from the US government's dealings with the Sioux, starting in 1868. Refer to Phases 4 and 5 to help you.

We are **part of the earth** – we came from the earth and will return to the earth.

PHASE 1, 1825–1840: INDIAN LAND

1834 – The Great Plains were declared Indian country. Non-Indians were not interested in this land.

PHASE 2, 1840–1850: PASSING THROUGH

The different groups that you studied in Chapter 2 – the pioneers, Mormons and gold miners – all began to head west during this period.

We have come to buy and farm **our own** land. This is our Manifest Destiny.

PHASE 3, 1850–1859: SETTLING IN

People began to settle on the Great Plains and were encouraged to move west by the government.

In **1851** the Fort Laramie Treaty was passed which defined the areas in which the Indians could hunt. It also gave travellers a route across the Great Plains.

Opinion on what to do about the 'Indian problem' was divided: the NEGOTIATORS wanted a settlement that was sensitive to the Plains Indians and their way of life. The EXTERMINATORS saw the Indians as savages.

We will fight to protect ourselves and to uphold the treaties we had to sign.

We will fight for **our** land.

PHASE 4, 1859–1869: CONFLICT

This was a period of great conflict between the Indians and the settlers with wars, battles and massacres being fought, such as the Sand Creek Massacre in 1864.

In **1865** Red Cloud's War started – you will find out about this on page 72.

In **1868** the second Fort Laramie Treaty was signed as the first had been broken. This Treaty created the Great Sioux Reservation – an area which non-Indians could not enter.

PHASE 5, 1869–1878: DEFEAT

There were more conflicts between Indian nations and non-Indians in this period.

In **1874** gold was discovered in the Black Hills and miners flooded onto Indian land. The miners were then attacked by the Indians.

In **1876** the Great Sioux War began.

June 1876 – the Battle of the Little Big Horn. Despite winning the battle, the Sioux lost the war and were forced to surrender.

PHASE 6, 1878–1890: END OF A WAY OF LIFE

The end of the Plains Indians' way of life was brought about by:
- the destruction of the buffalo herds
- the resettlement of all Indian nations onto reservations, by 1885.

In **1890** the frontier was declared closed.

Was the US army well-prepared to fight the Indians?

Weaknesses

> The worst thing about fighting Indians is that they don't stand and fight like men. They ambush their enemies and then run away if outnumbered. Like my company commander says, when you fight Indians the front is all around and the rear is nowhere.

> The worst thing is the life we have to live. Our food is poor and our living conditions are terrible. These uniforms are cheap and useless in the incredibly cold winter weather. Fighting Indians is our only excitement, if we could only find them. On patrol we can go days and days without seeing a single Indian. We are in greater danger of dying from disease than from fighting Indians.

> The worst thing is the poor quality of the men. So many of them are unwilling to work and drunkenness is a major problem. I'm sure some of them are on the run from the law back east or in their home countries. I read a letter in the *Army and Navy Journal* recently where a captain complained about the different nationalities of his recruits and having to talk to them in French, German and even Arabic!

> I agree. The recruits are a poor lot and DESERTION is another big problem. When I was serving with Custer in the Seventh CAVALRY there were deserters riding away every night.

Strengths

Despite their weaknesses the US army also had some advantages over the Indians.

Forts
The forts in the West were built to protect travellers and to control reservations. They acted as a safe base from which the army could patrol and attack the Indians. Protected by walls and armed with men and artillery, they were far too strong for Indians to attack successfully.

■ **DISCUSS**

Why do you think men deserted from the US army on the Plains?

Indian scouts

Indian scouts were recruited from different Indian nations. They were quite willing to fight alongside the US army against their traditional enemies. So, for example, Custer's Crow Indian scouts were happy to fight against their traditional enemies, the Sioux. Their knowledge of the country and Sioux battle tactics was invaluable.

The end of the Civil War in 1865

When the Civil War ended hundreds of regular soldiers, led by experienced officers, became available to deal with the Indians. They replaced the volunteer soldiers who had been at best ineffective and at worst guilty of atrocities. The worst example was the Sand Creek Massacre of 1864 when a peaceful Cheyenne village was attacked by volunteer soldiers and 105 women and children were killed alongside 28 men.

New strategies

1 **Total war** was first used by General Sheridan in the Civil War. It meant to wage war on the whole enemy population, not just their soldiers. It did not mean killing women and children, but destroying all the food, shelter, clothing and horses of the Plains Indians. This left them with a choice between starvation or surrendering and living on the reservation.

2 **Winter campaigns** were very effective. The Plains Indians were vulnerable to attack in winter. With heavy snow and sub-zero temperatures they needed to stay in one place and conserve their food supplies and the strength of their horses. Defeat at this time of year could be devastating.

▼ **SOURCE 1** A photograph of Curley, Custer's Crow Indian scout who survived the Battle of the Little Big Horn

▼ **SOURCE 2** A photograph of General Philip Henry Sheridan, Commander in Chief of the army of the West. He planned the Little Big Horn campaign

■ ACTIVITY

Write a paragraph to explain how the following factors strengthened the US army's ability to fight the Sioux:

- forts
- Indian scouts
- the end of the Civil War
- new strategies.

When you answer this type of question it is important to write a paragraph that deals with **each** factor and where possible **the links between them**. Here you could make a link between the end of the Civil War and the use of the new strategies by experienced officers against the Indians.

4.2 *Case study: the Battle of the Little Big Horn*

The Battle of the Little Big Horn was the biggest victory for the Plains Indians. You will examine the events and weigh up the evidence to decide how far Colonel Custer was to blame for the US defeat.

▶ **SOURCE 1**
A photograph of Sitting Bull

Why did the Sioux go to war?

Red Cloud's War 1865–1868

In 1862 gold was discovered in the Rocky Mountains of Montana. New mining towns sprang up and miners travelled across Sioux lands. This broke the **Fort Laramie Peace Treaty** signed in 1851, which defined the Indians' land. The Sioux responded by attacking any miners and travellers entering their lands. Then the US army moved in to build forts to protect the miners and travellers. The Sioux, under the leadership of Red Cloud, now attacked the army. The Sioux could not capture the forts, but they could, and did, stop the US army moving freely outside them.

Meanwhile, a new trail had been opened to the mining areas. So the government admitted defeat and changed its policy. A new Fort Laramie Treaty was signed in 1868. The US government agreed to abandon the forts and the Great Sioux Reservation was created. Non-Indians would never be allowed to enter this Sioux land.

The Great Sioux War 1876–1877

Causes

In 1874 an expedition of the Seventh Cavalry, led by George Armstrong Custer, discovered gold in the Black Hills. This expedition broke the Fort Laramie Treaty of 1868. Once the news broke miners flooded into the Black Hills. The army was unable, and the government was unwilling, to stop them. The Sioux were outraged. The Black Hills were sacred. The miners were attacked.

The government now tried to buy the Black Hills from the Sioux. Their offer of 6 million dollars was rejected because the Sioux believed that no one could own the land. Relations between the government and the Sioux were now very poor.

In December 1875 the government went further. They ordered all the Sioux onto the reservation. Several thousand Sioux, who lived in the Powder River country and were led by Sitting Bull and Crazy Horse, refused to live on the reservation. However, even if they had wanted to obey this order, in winter they could not have travelled through the snow.

■ **DISCUSS**

Why did the government have to keep changing its approach to the Indians?

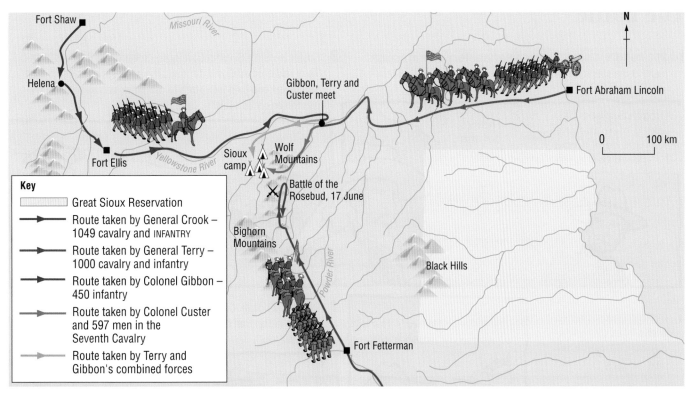

Key
- Great Sioux Reservation
- Route taken by General Crook – 1049 cavalry and INFANTRY
- Route taken by General Terry – 1000 cavalry and infantry
- Route taken by Colonel Gibbon – 450 infantry
- Route taken by Colonel Custer and 597 men in the Seventh Cavalry
- Route taken by Terry and Gibbon's combined forces

▲ **SOURCE 2** A map of the Little Big Horn campaign

The campaign plan

In February 1876 the US army was ordered to attack any Sioux who had not returned to the reservation. General Sheridan devised a plan. Three separate COLUMNS led by General Crook, Colonel Gibbon and General Terry would trap the Sioux. The plan had two key weaknesses:

- there was no effective communication between the columns
- there was no serious attempt to find out Indian numbers. The army believed there were 800 warriors. In fact, there were about 2000.

■ DISCUSS

1 Whose fault was it that the plan had weaknesses?
2 Why do you think that some Sioux were better armed than the soldiers?
3 What would the effect of Crook's defeat be on:
  a) the plan **b)** the Sioux's morale?

Things begin to go wrong – the Battle of the Rosebud

On 17 June General Crook's column had stopped for a coffee break when Crazy Horse attacked with about 1500 warriors. Instead of their usual hit-and-run tactics, Crazy Horse led his warriors in repeated attacks all day. Many Indian warriors with their Winchester repeating rifles were better armed than the cavalrymen with their single-shot Springfield rifles!

By nightfall 28 of Crook's men had been killed and 63 wounded. His men had fired 25,000 rounds of ammunition. The Indians' casualties were believed to be 36 dead and 63 wounded, but Crook had been defeated. The next day he retreated south towards Fort Fetterman. The victorious Crazy Horse took his forces to join with Sitting Bull on the Little Big Horn, creating a combined force of over 2000 warriors.

Meanwhile, to the north, the remaining two columns led by Terry and Gibbon met on the Yellowstone River.

The Battle

1 21 June 1876. Colonel Custer and General Terry meet to discuss plans at the junction of the Yellowstone River and Rosebud Creek.

2 Custer leads his Seventh Cavalry south along the Rosebud Creek. Terry had ordered Custer to round the southern edge of the Wolf Mountains and then turn north to catch the Indians between their two forces on 26 June.

3 Custer's cavalry covered twelve miles on the first day, then 60 miles in the next two days.

4 Evening, 24 June. Custer decides on a change of plan, to follow a fresh Indian trail over the Wolf Mountains in a night march.

5 10-mile night march.

6 Daybreak, 25 June. Custer's cavalry has arrived a day early.

7 Midday, 25 June. Custer's scouts report that the Indians seem to be packing up and leaving. Custer divides his force into three attacking sections commanded by himself, Major Reno and Captain Benteen.

8

I can give you 180 extra men and the GATLING GUNS if you need them.

Thanks, but my Seventh Cavalry are enough and the Gatling guns would only slow me down.

What's the rush for?

Custer wants to beat the Indians all by himself, before Terry gets there!

We advance at once.

Indian village 15 miles away on the Little Big Horn. Many, many *tipis*.

Why do you allow your men to light fires? The smoke will give us away.

The largest Indian camp on the North American continent is ahead, and I am going to attack it.

I warned him. If we go in there we will never come out.

US 7

260 Men

125 Men

125 Men

9 25 June, 3.00p.m. While Custer rides north, Major Reno attacks the village from the south.

10 Reno's force meets fierce opposition from the Sioux and their allies.

There are too many of them. Get back!

11 25 June, 4.00p.m. Reno, now joined by Benteen, retreats to the high ground and digs in.

Where is Custer?

Wherever he is we can't help him, not faced by this many Indians.

12 25 June, 3.00p.m. Meanwhile, Custer and his men approach the Indian village, but are met with opposition.

Take a message to Captain Benteen. Ride as fast as you can and tell him to hurry. Tell him to bring the ammunition packs as soon as possible.

13 With Reno on the defensive many Sioux, led by Crazy Horse, turn their attack on Custer.

Sir, we must pull back, there are thousands of them.

14 Custer leads his men in a retreat. They try to get to the high ground to make a stand. But Crazy Horse gets there first and his warriors close in.

They've got better guns than us!

■ DISCUSS

Custer was later accused of making a number of military mistakes in the five days leading up to the battle of the Little Big Horn. These were that he:

■ refused reinforcements
■ pushed his men too hard
■ divided his command
■ attacked the enemy without having good intelligence of their numbers.

1 Can you find evidence to support these accusations in this cartoon strip?
2 Can you suggest any other reasons for the US army's defeat?

Interpreting the Battle of the Little Big Horn

This battle was the worst defeat of the US army by the Plains Indians. Custer and 262 of his officers and men were killed. Of the survivors under the command of Major Reno, 52 were wounded. Since then the battle, often called Custer's Last Stand, has been used as a subject by many artists. It has been painted more than 950 times. Sources 3 and 4 are two paintings that give very different versions of the battle.

▼ **SOURCE 3** Edgar Paxson's painting, *Custer's Last Battle*. It was finished in 1893 after six years of research, including a visit to the battlefield and interviews with survivors from both sides

▲ **SOURCE 4** Eric von Schmidt's painting, *Here Fell Custer*, completed in 1976 and based on years of historical research. This is considered to be the most accurate portrayal of the battle and the battlefield. It is the painting used by the US National Park service on their battlefield leaflet

■ **ACTIVITY**

You will need to use all of your source analysis skills in this Activity! Study the details in Sources 3 and 4 very carefully and answer the following questions.

1 Who is shown in the centre of each painting? Compare these two characters. What are they holding? How are they standing?
2 How are the soldiers of the Seventh Cavalry presented in each source? What are they doing? How many of them are still alive?
3 How are the Indians shown in each source? Where are they? What are they doing?
4 Can you find the bugler in each painting? Is he dead or alive?
5 One painting shows the Indian village. Where do you think it is? How big is it?
6 From what viewpoint has each artist painted the battle?
7 Choose one word or phrase to describe the death of Custer and his men shown in each painting.
8 There are similarities and differences between these two paintings. Which painting do you think best helps you to understand what happened in the battle? Explain your answer.

Was Custer to blame for the defeat at the Battle of the Little Big Horn?

News of the disaster at the Little Big Horn reached the rest of America on 4 July, the hundredth anniversary of the USA's independence. Americans were shocked. Many people blamed Custer. Others blamed Reno for not supporting Custer. An inquiry was held to decide who was responsible for the defeat.

The Little Big Horn Inquiry

▼ **SOURCE 5** An extract from a letter written by First Lieutenant Holmes O. Paulding on 28 June 1876. Paulding, an assistant surgeon serving with General Terry, was writing from the battlefield to reassure his mother that he was safe

The trouble with Custer was he did not know what he was attacking and failed to surprise the camp. So when he was moving along concealed the Indians seem to have outflanked and surrounded them. More than half of that gallant regiment is dead, among them several dear friends of mine – Custer, Cook, Keogh, Jack Sturgis, Porter, Yates, Tom and Boss Custer and all the other poor fellows. Among them too was my old friend Dr Geo Lord. About 300 or 350 dead and 50 badly wounded of Reno's outfit. After driving Reno onto the bluffs after the massacre of Custer's battalion, the Indians surrounded him and fought from all sides all day of the 26th. About dark we were seen coming up the valley eight or ten miles off. When we went into camp that night the Indians ran away.

▼ **SOURCE 6** Captain Frederick Benteen, who had hated Custer for years, speaking at the inquiry

Custer disobeyed orders because he did not want any other command or commander to have a finger in the pie … and thereby lost his life.

▼ **SOURCE 7** Major Reno speaking at the inquiry

Well sir, I had known General Custer a long time and I had no confidence in his ability as a soldier.

▼ **SOURCE 8** President Ulysses S. Grant in a newspaper interview in 1876. Custer had accused the President's brother of corruption

I regard Custer's massacre as a sacrifice of troops, brought on by Custer himself.

▼ **SOURCE 9** The historian Stephen Ambrose writing in his book, *Crazy Horse and Custer: The Parallel Lives of Two American Warriors*, 1975

Crazy Horse took in the situation with a glance, then acted with great decisiveness. He fought with his usual reckless bravery, providing as always an example for the other warriors to admire, draw courage from, and emulate [imitate], but his real contribution to this greatest of Indian victories was mental, not physical. His outstanding generalship had brought him at the head of a ferocious body of warriors to the critical point at the critical moment. Then with his courage he took advantage of the situation to sweep down on Custer.

■ **ACTIVITY**

Study Sources 5–9. Then look back over pages 72–78 and copy and complete the table below to record how the various actions of each person or group contributed to the defeat of the US army at the Little Big Horn.

	The actions of:				
	Custer	Custer's subordinates	Custer's superiors	The Sioux and their allies	Others
Planning the campaign					
During the campaign					
At the battle					

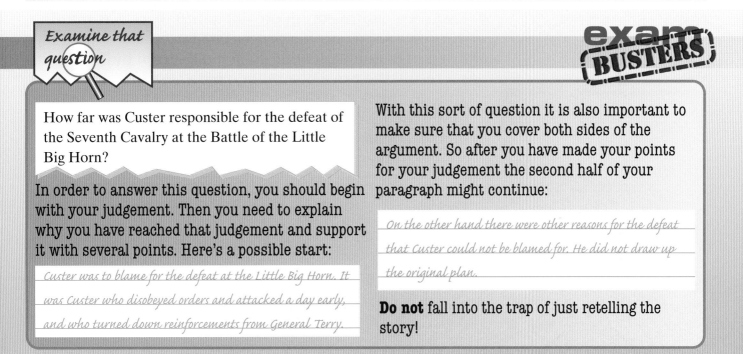

Examine that question

examp BUSTERS

How far was Custer responsible for the defeat of the Seventh Cavalry at the Battle of the Little Big Horn?

In order to answer this question, you should begin with your judgement. Then you need to explain why you have reached that judgement and support it with several points. Here's a possible start:

Custer was to blame for the defeat at the Little Big Horn. It was Custer who disobeyed orders and attacked a day early, and who turned down reinforcements from General Terry.

With this sort of question it is also important to make sure that you cover both sides of the argument. So after you have made your points for your judgement the second half of your paragraph might continue:

On the other hand there were other reasons for the defeat that Custer could not be blamed for. He did not draw up the original plan.

Do not fall into the trap of just retelling the story!

Why did the Indians lose the war?
The military response to the Little Big Horn was overwhelming. Two new forts were built on the Yellowstone and 2500 reinforcements sent west. After the battle the Indians split up again into their small bands in search of food and grazing for their horses. Some returned to the reservation. The rest were followed and attacked throughout the autumn and winter.

The Indians were hopelessly outnumbered. They had to fight the US army while also trying to protect their women and children. They were short of ammunition and food. One by one the bands were forced to surrender and return to the reservation.

On 5 May 1877 Crazy Horse and his band surrendered. On the same day Sitting Bull and his band escaped to Canada.

4.3 *Why did the Indians lose control of the Plains?*

After winning a military victory against the Sioux the US government set out to 'solve the Indian Problem for good'. You will find out how hunting the buffalo and creating the reservations helped them do this. For your final task you will consider the bigger picture, and use cards to work out how many different factors worked together to end the Indian control of the Plains.

▼ **SOURCE 1** Buffalo skulls piled by the railroad, 1880s

The buffalo

In 1840 there were an estimated 13 million buffalo. By 1885 there were just 200 animals left. The main reason for this dramatic fall in numbers was hunting. In 1871 a tanning process had been discovered that allowed high quality leather to be made from buffalo hides. As a result, the price of a buffalo hide shot up. At the same time the arrival of the railroads allowed hunters to flood onto the Plains to shoot the buffalo. The same railroads then carried the hides back east to the tanneries. By 1875 buffalo hunters had wiped out the southern buffalo herd. After the arrival of the Northern Pacific Railroad at Bismarck in 1876, and the military defeat of the Sioux in 1877, the northern buffalo herd was next. In 1882 an estimated 5000 hunters and skinners were at work on the northern plains. By 1885 the northern herd was gone.

■ ACTIVITY

According to the historian Richard White, hunting was not the only reason for the end of the buffalo. He argued that buffalo numbers were already in trouble by 1840 for four reasons:

- the destruction of its habitat by settlers
- drought
- competition for grass with Indian horses
- diseases brought by the cattle of settlers.

Other historians argue that the destruction of the buffalo was a deliberate US government policy. They point to the fact that in 1874 the US Congress passed a bill to try to protect the buffalo but President Grant refused to sign the bill so it could not become law.

1 Study Sources 2–5. Your teacher can give you copies. All four sources make exactly the same point to explain why the US government would be happy if the buffalo were destroyed. What is it? Highlight where it appears in each source.
2 Write one sentence for each source to summarise the author's views of the destruction of the buffalo.
3 Why would the US government be happy that the buffalo were wiped out?

▼ **SOURCE 2** Tall Boy, a Cheyenne chief, talking to General Winfield Scott Hancock in 1867

The buffalo are diminishing [reducing in number] fast. When they all die we shall be hungry; we shall want something to eat, and we will be forced to come into the fort.

▼ **SOURCE 3** General Philip H. Sheridan describing the work of the buffalo hunters in 1873

These men have done more in the last two years, and will do more in the next year to settle the ... Indian question, than the entire regular army has done in the last 30 years. They are destroying the Indians' food supply ... let them kill, skin and sell until the buffaloes are exterminated.

▼ **SOURCE 4** Teddy 'Blue' Abbott, a cowboy in the 1880s

The buffalo slaughter was a dirty business ... a put-up job on the part of the government to control Indians by getting rid of their food supply.

▼ **SOURCE 5** Frank Mayer, a buffalo hunter, 1873

I would ride into one of the army camps on a Sunday morning and seek an interview with the commanding officer. We would sit and smoke. After a while he would ask if I could use some ammunition. Sure I could. Whereupon as much as I could carry was all mine. I was young and callow [inexperienced] in those days and thought it was my good looks or winning personality which was making the army so generous to me.

Later I asked an officer, 'What am I expected to do with this ammunition – kill Indians?'

'Hell no, that's our job', replied the officer. 'You must kill buffalo. We'll take care of the Indians. Mayer, either the buffalo or the Indian must go. There isn't any other way. Only when the Indian becomes absolutely dependent upon us for his every need will we be able to handle him. Every buffalo you kill will save a white man's life. Go to it.'

Reservations

The system of Indian reservations was developed from 1825 onwards. The government plan was to keep Indians separate from the ranchers and homesteaders. The Indians were to be supervised by government-appointed INDIAN AGENTS. They were expected to live as farmers. To begin with the Indians were allowed to leave the reservation to hunt the buffalo, but after the wars of the 1860s and 1870s this was no longer allowed.

Conditions on the reservations were bad. Often the land was poor farming land, unwanted by the settlers. And the Indians were hunters not farmers. This made it difficult for the Indians to feed themselves and they became dependent upon government rations of food and clothing. Individual people were punished for offences without trial and some were killed. The two famous leaders Sitting Bull and Crazy Horse were both killed on the Sioux reservation, in each case whilst being arrested.

For a society based upon hunting and war and moving freely across the Plains, life on handouts on the reservation was demoralising. There was no way in which a warrior could gain or maintain status. Disarmed, without their horses, poorly fed and sometimes suffering from diseases such as measles, influenza and whooping cough, the Indians were unable to fight back.

▼ **SOURCE 6** A government agent distributing food rations to the Sioux

Within the reservations the US government followed a deliberate policy of destroying all aspects of Indian culture. This policy had five strands:

1 Territorial

Through a series of laws the Sioux reservation was reduced and the Sioux were split into smaller groups.

▼ **SOURCE 7** Three maps showing the break-up of the Great Sioux Reservation, 1868–1890

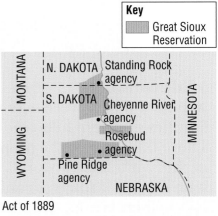

Key

Great Sioux Reservation

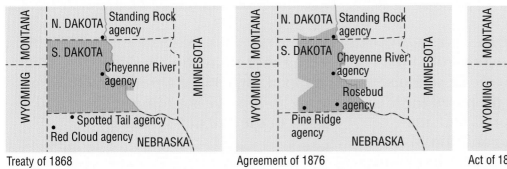

Treaty of 1868   Agreement of 1876   Act of 1889

2 Political

At first rations were distributed through the chiefs. Then the heads of individual families were encouraged to collect their own rations. This was a deliberate step to weaken the authority of chiefs.

The **Dawes General Allotment Act** was passed in 1887. This did two things.

- Firstly, it allowed the shared Indian land to be broken up into individual plots. Again this was a deliberate step to weaken the tribal structure and the power of chiefs.
- Secondly, it allowed any land that was left over to be sold to non-Indians, an opportunity for land grabbers to make money.

3 Economic

The ban on the Sioux leaving the reservation to hunt or make war on their enemies destroyed the economic foundation of their society. There were no buffalo to provide food, shelter and clothing and no stolen horses to add to their wealth.

■ ACTIVITY

Your task is to make a set of bullet point notes using the five numbered headings on pages 83 and 84 that explain how reservations controlled the Plains Indians by destroying their culture. For each heading you should write only two or three bullet points. One has been done for you.

Economic
- No hunting meant no buffalo for food, clothing and shelter
- No war meant ...

4 Religious

Feasts, dances and ceremonies like the Sun Dance were banned. The power of medicine men was deliberately undermined. With their new way of life the Indians had no need to call on the spirits for help in hunting and war. As Indian beliefs declined Christian missionaries moved in to fill the spiritual gap.

■ ACTIVITY

1 Study Sources 8A and 8B. Find as many changes as you can between the boys in the two photographs.
2 How would each of the following people have felt about these changes:
   a) the boys themselves
   b) their parents
   c) the man who ran the school?

5 Educational

Indian children were taken from their families and sent to boarding schools. There they were to be prepared for life in the 'white man's world'. One man who ran a boarding school said his aim for each child was to 'Kill the Indian in him and save the man'. Indian children were not allowed to speak their own language. They were taught to have no respect for their traditional way of life. If parents tried to stop their children being sent away their rations were stopped. By 1887, 2020 Indian children were in the 117 boarding schools and 2500 in the 110 day schools.

▲ **SOURCE 8** Three Sioux boys at the Carlisle Indian Boarding School. They were photographed as new arrivals (A) and then again six months later (B)

The Ghost Dance Movement

In 1889 an Indian holy man, Wovoka, had a vision. His vision said that if the Indians danced the Ghost Dance then a new world would come. The whites would disappear and the buffalo would return.

On the Sioux Reservation conditions were bad. The Sioux's rations had been cut and the drought of 1890 led their crops to fail. In this climate of despair hundreds took up the Ghost Dance. This scared the Indian agents who tried to ban the Ghost Dance. When this failed they called in the US army. An attempt to arrest Sitting Bull ended with him being killed. This just made the situation worse.

In this tense atmosphere the soldiers of the Seventh Cavalry took into custody Chief Big Foot (another chief leading the Dance) and his followers, at Wounded Knee.

On 29 December 1890, when the soldiers moved to disarm the Sioux, a shot was fired and fighting broke out. The soldiers were prepared for trouble and opened fire with repeating rifles and four cannon. By the time the firing stopped 25 soldiers and 146 Sioux were dead. The Sioux dead consisted of 102 adult men and women, 24 old men, seven old women, six boys between the ages of five and eight and seven babies under the age of two.

This massacre marked the end of the Plains Wars. To the Sioux it also marked another end. One survivor, Black Elk, wrote:

'When I look back now from this high hill of my old age, I can still see the butchered women and children lying heaped and scattered all along the crooked ditch as plain as I saw them with eyes still young. And I can see something else died there in that bloody mud, and was buried in the blizzard. A people's dream died there. It was a beautiful dream. The Nation's hoop is broken and scattered. There is no centre any longer and the sacred tree is dead.'

■ DISCUSS

1 What does Black Elk mean when he uses the words, the 'beautiful dream'?
2 Do you think Wounded Knee was a bloody massacre or a tragic accident of war?

▲ **SOURCE 9** The Sioux dead being buried in a mass grave at Wounded Knee. Civilian labourers did the work, guarded by soldiers

■ **ACTIVITY**

Why did the Indians lose control of the Plains?

1 This is a very important historical question. In order to help you to answer it you need to make a set of cause cards.
Each card should include no more than two bullet points, like the one below.
Use the information on these two pages to help you.

> MANIFEST DESTINY
> • America should occupy the whole continent
> • Indians were in the way

Use your cause cards to complete the following tasks:

a) Group the cards into different types of cause – economic, political and military. You could colour code these.

b) Next draw a Venn diagram like the one shown here and try to fit the cause cards into it. What does this tell you about the causes?

c) Can you find any other ways of grouping the cards?

d) Now sort them in order of importance.

2 Finally, decide on what you think is the best way of arranging the cause cards to answer the question: 'Why did the Indians lose control of the Plains?'. Take a large sheet of paper and stick them down. If you think you need to draw any lines to link causes or if you need to write any explanation then do so to finish your answer.

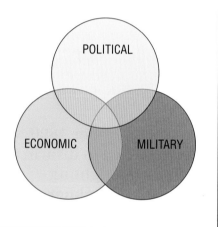

MANIFEST DESTINY
Americans believed in their Manifest Destiny to occupy the whole country from coast to coast. This was their justification for all of their actions, even treating the Indians badly.

US GOVERNMENT POLICY
The US government usually supported the miners, homesteaders and ranchers against the Indians. When the sides came into conflict the government sent in the US army to deal with the 'Indian Problem'.

CATTLE RANCHING
Ranchers grazed their cattle on the land where the buffalo used to graze and the Plains Indians used to live. They wanted the Plains Indians kept on the reservations.

GOLD
Miners digging for gold in the Black Hills in 1874 were on Plains Indian land, breaking the Fort Laramie Treaty. Unable, or unwilling, to remove the miners, the government instead sent in the US army to protect them from the Plains Indians.

THE END OF THE AMERICAN CIVIL WAR IN 1865
The US government could now concentrate on the West. Money was available to build railroads and to encourage settlers. Many people, like freed slaves and ex-soldiers, were keen to move west to settle and start a new life.

HOMESTEADING
Homesteaders fenced off land for farming – land that the buffalo used to graze on, and the Plains Indians used to live on. Whenever there was trouble the homesteaders demanded that the government force the Plains Indians onto reservations.

RESERVATIONS
The system of reservations kept Plains Indians under control and destroyed their culture. By taking away their horses and weapons the government made them dependent on handouts which could be taken away for 'bad' behaviour.

US ARMY
The US army's huge manpower was too strong for the Plains Indians to fight. The system of forts gave them control of the Plains and the strategies of total war and winter campaigns were decisive in winning a military victory.

PLAINS INDIAN WEAPONS AND TACTICS
Plains Indians were used to warfare as a series of small raids in which warriors fought as individuals. They were unwilling to suffer heavy losses and unable to replace their losses. On the whole they were less well armed than the US army.

DIVISIONS BETWEEN INDIAN NATIONS
The tradition of warfare on the Plains meant that the Plains Indians were never able to unite to fight the US army. Some nations, such as the Crow, fought alongside the US army against their traditional enemies the Sioux.

RAILROADS
The railroads opened up the West to the homesteaders, ranchers and buffalo hunters. Without the railroads they would not have been there. The railroads also supplied the US army's forts and moved its soldiers quickly.

DESTRUCTION OF THE BUFFALO
The destruction of the buffalo took away the vital support for the Plains Indians' way of life. Without the economic basis of their society they could not exist on the Plains.

PLAINS INDIAN SOCIETY
The Plains Indians were never able to fight a long campaign against the army. They had their families to feed and protect and their way of life depended upon them roaming the Plains in small groups.

Examine that
question

1 How was the way of life of the Plains Indian suited to the Great Plains?

(4 marks)

3 How far was Custer responsible for the defeat of the Seventh Cavalry at the Battle of the Little Big Horn? (12 marks)

2 Why was there conflict between the Plains Indians and the Americans?

(10 marks)

These are the types of question that are likely to appear in your GCSE examination. Let's take each of them in turn and see what the examiner is looking for in your answers.

1 The first question is quite straightforward. Notice that it is worth only a few marks. This means that you are not expected to write a long answer. What is important is that you **select** two or three points that are **relevant to the question**.

Think back to the set of revision cards you made on page 18. These can help you to write a good answer to this question, but you do not need to write about all five factors. Write your own answer to this question using just two or three examples.

2 The second question is more important. 'Why' questions are very common in GCSE exams and they carry a lot of marks. To answer them well you must remember to do four things:

- **Plan** your answer before you begin writing.
- **Make connections!** Chapter 2 was about the settlement of the West, Chapter 4 was about a related topic, the defeat of the Indians. You need to pull in information from both of these to help plan your answer.
- You cannot write about all of the reasons for conflict. Again, you need to **select** two or three important reasons.
- **Explain!** This question requires an explanation, not a description. You need to explain the reasons why there was conflict between the Plains Indians and the Americans.

!
WARNING

WHY = PLAN/CONNECT/
SELECT/EXPLAIN

Read the student's answer on page 89. How could you improve it? Use the examiner's comments to rewrite the student's answer.

Improve that answer

There was conflict between the Plains Indians and the settlers because of travellers crossing the Plains and the homesteaders and cattlemen. This made the Indians mad especially when the buffalo were shot. The US army beat the Indians, although in one famous battle at the Little Big Horn, Colonel Custer got what he deserved when he and his men were killed. They did not like the reservations. Manifest Destiny caused conflict as well. White settlers said God was on their side.

The student has written too little. The student has selected from the evidence, but has failed to explain or make connections. Some parts of the answer are irrelevant.

3 The third question is tricky. Like an iceberg, there is more to this question than what appears on the surface. The danger is that you write about only Custer. This would be very dangerous. Look at the question closely. You are being asked to explain **how far** Custer was responsible for losing the battle. To do this you must look at the actions of other people as well.

Use the advice shown above to write an essay to answer question 3.

Step 1: Deal with the part of the question that is above the surface.
- Explain how Custer was anxious to claim all the glory for himself and attacked the Indian camp without waiting for support.
- Point out his military mistakes – refusing reinforcements, attacking with tired men, splitting up his forces.

Step 2: Deal with the part of the question that lurks beneath the surface. You could include:
- The weakness in General Sheridan's plan.
- The fighting ability of the Sioux.
- The fact that some of the Sioux were better armed than the seventh cavalry.
- What Reno and Benteen did and did not do.

Step 3: Write your conclusion. DO NOT SIT ON THE FENCE! The question asks how far Custer was responsible so say what you think. How important were the other people involved? Make sure you support your answer with what you know.

Remember, other historians still argue about this question.

The overall picture: what have you learned?

■ ACTIVITY

At the beginning of this book (see page 3) we asked you to choose a good image to go with each of the four investigations. Now is the time for you to collect together your ideas.

1 Take each of your chosen images in turn. Write a caption for each one. Then explain your choice.
2 Now look at the front cover. Is this a good image, or can you think of a better one? Explain your choice.

> *It has helped me to understand what it means to be human, because we have been looking at the lives and beliefs of real people.*

> *Studying the American West has helped me to get better at history, by using sources and explaining why things happen.*

> *It is important because the history of the American West is still relevant today. That is shown by the argument about pardoning Billy the Kid.*

■ DISCUSS

3 Each of the students here is suggesting reasons why we should study the American West. Which do you think is the most convincing?
4 What else have you learned from this depth study?

> *It has taught me the danger of thinking that our culture is the only correct way of living, and the value of understanding other peoples' cultures.*

Putting it all together

This book has suggested some techniques you could use to help you revise. Here is a reminder of two of them.

■ ACTIVITY 1

On pages 46–47 you created a memory map for the homesteaders. You can use this technique to help you to understand and remember a number of other topics. For example, here is one that we have started on the Mormons. The question is:

> How successful were the Mormon leaders?

We have completed the boughs and branches for Joseph Smith showing his successes and failures. Your task is to complete the boughs and branches for Brigham Young to show his successes and failures. Try to make as many connections between different factors as you can.

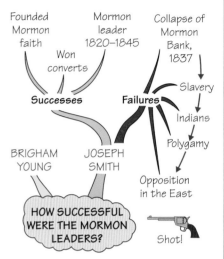

■ ACTIVITY 2

On page 58 you made a set of Top Trumps cards, based on the different types of crime. Now try to make a set for the different groups in the American West who had an impact on the lives of the Plains Indians. You will need to include each of the following:

- Mountain men
- Gold miners
- Homesteaders
- Railroad builders
- US army officers
- Buffalo hunters
- Pioneers
- Mormons
- Cattlemen and cowboys
- US cavalrymen
- Indian school principals

Here are our suggestions for the categories you could score each group on, out of 10.

Group:	Score
How much land they took from the Plains Indians	/10
How much damage they did to the Plains Indians' food supplies	/10
How much harm they did to the Plains Indians' way of life	/10
How big an impact they had on the Plains Indians	/10

AMERICAN CIVIL WAR the war between the slave-owning Southern (Confederate) states and the Northern (Unionist) states of the USA, which lasted from 1861 to 1865

BAND a small group of Plains Indians made up of several families

BARBED WIRE spiked steel wire ideal for fencing, invented in 1874 by Joseph Glidden

BARREN land too poor to grow food on

BUGLE a brass instrument like a trumpet used to give military signals

BULL BOAT a light boat made from buffalo hides, stretched across a wooden frame

CATTLE BARON a powerful cattle rancher who owns a lot of land and many cattle

CATTLE BRANDING burning a mark into the hide of cattle to mark their ownership

CATTLE DRIVE moving cattle over a long distance on foot

CAVALRY soldiers who fight on horseback

CHUCK WAGON the wagon used to carry food and supplies for the cowboys on a cattle drive

CIVILISED someone or something which is advanced, refined or sophisticated

CLAIM an area of land that someone has claimed the right to own

CLAIM JUMPING stealing someone else's land or mining claim

COLUMN a group of people moving in rows, such as soldiers or pioneers

CONGREGATION the people watching and taking part in a religious ceremony

COWBOY a man who looked after cattle in the American West

DEPRESSION a period of time when the economy is weak and unemployment is high

DESERTION leaving a post without permission. It usually refers to soldiers

EMIGRATED left one country to settle in a new country

EXTERMINATOR someone who wanted to kill the Plains Indians

FORTY NINER a miner who took part in the Californian gold rush of 1849

FREE BLACKS ex-slaves from the Southern states of the USA

GATLING GUN a type of machine gun

GENTILE the name used by Mormons to describe non-Mormons

GRAIN BINDER a machine for tying wheat

HIDE the complete skin of an animal, usually a large animal such as the buffalo

INDIAN AGENT a US government official in charge of a reservation

INFANTRY soldiers who fight on foot

JURY the twelve men and women in a court of law who decide whether someone is innocent or guilty

LINCOLN COUNTY WAR this was a struggle between two rival groups of businessmen and ranchers. Murders and attacks between the two groups ended in a three-day battle in the town of Lincoln, New Mexico, during July 1878

LYNCHED unlawfully killed by being hanged by a mob, without a legal trial